# On Your Bike

## In and Around THE SURREY HILLS

**Valerie Bennett**
**Photographs by James Bennett**

COUNTRYSIDE BOOKS
NEWBURY BERKSHIRE

First published 2011




COUNTRYSIDE BOOKS
3 Catherine Road
Newbury, Berkshire

To view our complete range of books,
please visit us at
www.countrysidebooks.co.uk

ISBN 978 1 84674 232 3

Cover picture of Leith Hill
supplied by Derek Forss

Designed by Peter Davies, Nautilus Design
Maps by Gelder design and mapping

Produced through MRM Associates Ltd., Reading
Typeset by CJWT Solutions, St Helens
Printed in India

# CONTENTS

## AREA MAP SHOWING THE LOCATIONS OF THE RIDES

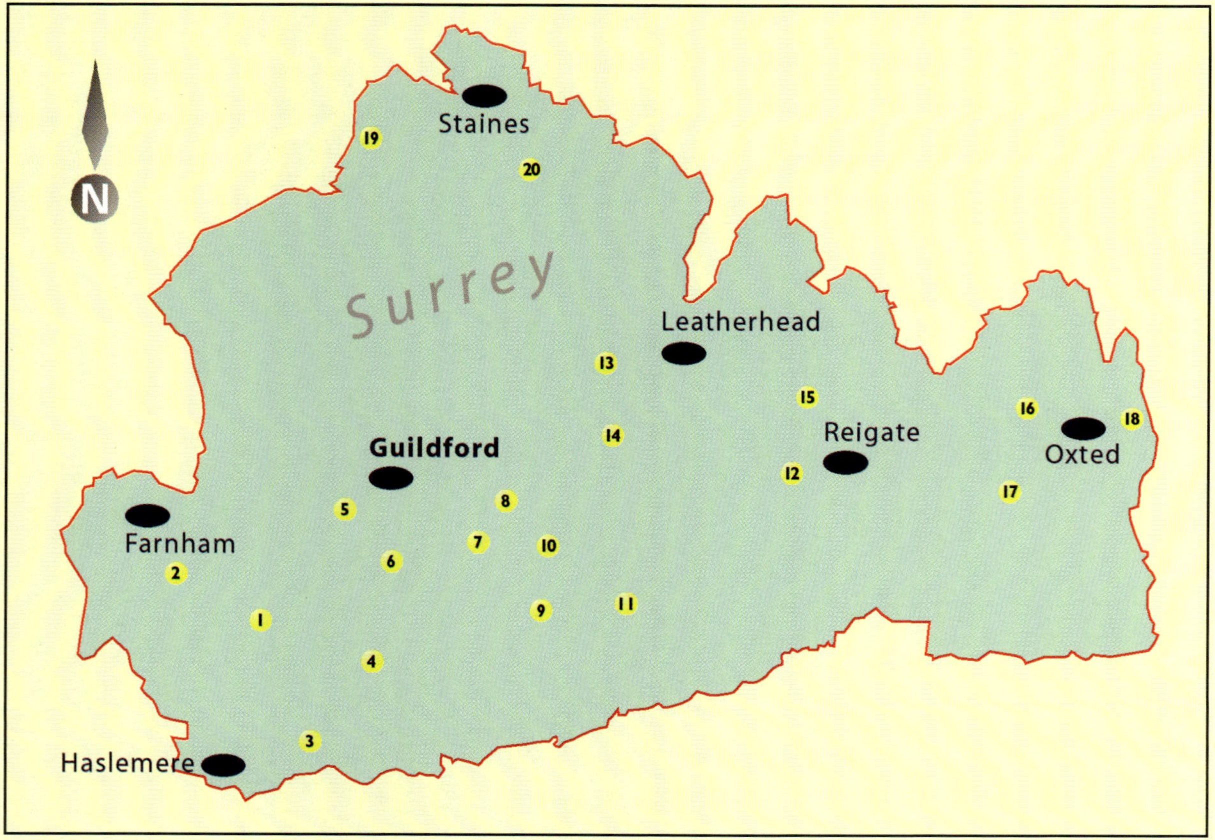

N
Surrey
Staines
Farnham
Haslemere
Guildford
Leatherhead
Reigate
Oxted
1 2 3 4 5 6 7 8 9 10 11 12 13 14 15 16 17 18 19 20

# INTRODUCTION

The Surrey Hills Area of Outstanding Natural Beauty covers a large swathe of the North Downs, from Farnham in the west to Limpsfield in the east, and encompasses many of the most scenic parts of Surrey. It includes well-known beauty spots with spectacular views such as Newlands Corner, Box Hill, Reigate Hill and, on the more southerly greensand ridge, the well-loved wooded hills of Pitch Hill, Holmbury Hill and Leith Hill. There is an abundance of leafy lanes, bridleways and footpaths, through glorious countryside, peppered with charming villages.

The aim of this guide is to help you to explore the Surrey Hills and surrounding areas by bicycle, with descriptions of rides from 9 to 33 miles. It is intended to be for everyone, from those starting or returning to cycling, to seasoned cyclists. Nineteen of the 20 routes are circular, whilst one along the Thames is linear. Some rides are almost entirely on quiet lanes whilst others include sections of straightforward, off-road riding away from traffic. This enables you to explore on peaceful paths in unspoilt countryside and offers the opportunity to see wildlife, ride through a nature reserve and follow a river bank. The routes are designed so that in fair weather conditions it should be possible to complete all of them without the need for an off-road bike.

The first guide *On Your Bike – Surrey* aimed to use the less hilly areas of the county, whereas this book includes a variety of terrain from flat rides to more challenging routes. Sometimes there is a longer hill but the effort is worthwhile for the panoramic views and exhilarating descents. There is usually countryside around you that can be enjoyed at a slower pace, so you can always get off your bike and push. Many will wish to take their time on these routes so that places of interest can be visited, the views enjoyed and stops made for refreshment at the many pubs and cafés along the way.

Cycling is a wonderful way of exploring this beautiful area with all it has to offer in the changing seasons. If you ride all of these routes, you should have a good overview of the Surrey Hills and the area surrounding them. Happy cycling in the Surrey countryside!

*Valerie Bennett*

# GUIDE TO USING THIS BOOK

Each route is preceded by information:

The total **number of miles** normally excludes detours, except where specified, e.g. route number 14.

The **introduction** to the ride gives a general outline of where the route goes and highlights points of interest along the way.

Using a **map** in conjunction with this guide is highly recommended. Ordnance Survey Landranger maps 1:50 000 can be used or OS Explorer maps 1:25 000 will offer more detail for off-road riding on bridleways.

Surrey County Council has an interactive map of the area with a wide choice of scales on their website. This is useful for viewing roads, paths and cycle routes, such as the Surrey Cycle Way, which can be overlaid on the map. The site is most easily found by using a search engine, and typing in 'Surrey interactive map'. Excellent Surrey Cycle Guide maps were available free to each of the eight areas of the county, but unfortunately there are now only a very limited number available. Try telephoning 03456 009 009 to obtain a copy.

The grid reference of the suggested **starting point** is given. This is usually a free car park where you can leave your car whilst you ride. Where a pub or garden centre car park is suggested, the owners have given permission in principle for guide users to park. However, landlords of pubs request that you ask first, in case there is a special function. They will appreciate it if you patronise their establishments, if only for drink.

Information regarding **cycling by train** can be obtained by telephoning National Rail Enquiries on 08457 48 49 50. Or try www.nationalrail.co.uk and look up 'Cycling by Train'. The nearest station(s) to the route have been given. Where possible, stations are on the route but sometimes it may be necessary to use a map to reach the route from the station of your choice.

A selection of pubs and tea rooms for **refreshment** are listed. Enjoy the pubs but don't forget paragraph 211 of the Highway Code. You must not ride under the influence of drink or drugs.

A **description of the route** is given to offer a guide to the sort of terrain and any traffic to expect. Most rides are on quiet lanes and many follow off-road bridleways but inevitably there are occasions when it is necessary to use busier roads for short sections.

## THE ROUTES

It is a good idea to read through the entire route before setting out so that you can see whether the ride is suitable for you, and to consider any additional options suggested.

Some directions have been **abbreviated:**
NCN is used for National Cycle Network where the routes are signed and numbered on a blue background. The NCN21 and NCN22 are used.
SP is used for 'signposted'.
SCW is Surrey Cycle Way, a signposted leisure route indicated by brown signs.
**Turn R** indicates that you turn right and **turn L**, turn left.

**Bridleways and footpaths:** Some rides are on bridleways and occasionally there may be a short section on a footpath. Bikes should be pushed on footpaths.

**Off-road paths** include canal and river towpaths and parks, where access may be permissive rather than a right of way. The authorities who manage these areas ask cyclists to ride with care and to give way to pedestrians.

The off-road routes in this book have been selected to be straightforward in fair weather conditions and all have been ridden by the author with a road bike. However, occasionally an uneven path may mean pushing your bike just a short distance, and any but the best of bridleways can be expected to have a few muddy patches following heavy rain or as winter approaches. Alternative road options have been suggested where the soil is less well drained, such as route 11 near Ockley.

**Shortened or extended rides:** Suggestions are given on some routes to help you to lengthen or shorten the ride.

**The Downs Link** near Guildford is used more than once as it is an excellent pathway, away from traffic. It offers easy access to Guildford and its surrounding areas, including the River Wey towpath.

## PREPARATION AND SAFETY

There are some common sense dos and don'ts for cyclists. The Cyclists' Touring Club offers a specialist service for the leisure cyclist for everything you need from buying a bike to insurance. A comprehensive guide is available on their website regarding cycling skills and tips. See their website www.ctc.org.uk or telephone 01483 238 337 for information.

Ensure that your bike is roadworthy and pay particular attention to your bike's brakes, gears and tyres. Take a spare inner tube or puncture repair kit, tyre levers and pump. A mobile phone may be useful in case of emergency. It is advisable to take a padlock with you in case you need to leave your bike unattended.

Wescott Cars (telephone: 01306 876968) have taxis with cycle racks. This can help with a pick-up in an emergency or to take you back to your starting point if you wish to undertake only part of a route.

On quiet lanes be prepared for a car coming towards you around the next corner. When riding off-road, be alert to pedestrians, horseriders and other potential hazards such as roots. Either fit your bike with a bell or call out to alert others of your presence.

Wear bright or light coloured clothes to make yourself more visible. Avoid clothing that could get tangled in the wheels or chain. Wearing a helmet is advisable. There is literature available on the subject from the Cyclists' Touring Club.

Take plenty of water to drink and any food you may need.

Having taken these precautions, you should be ready for your ride and to enjoy the spectacular countryside in and around the Surrey Hills.

# ACKNOWLEDGEMENTS

I would like to acknowledge the huge amount of help offered by the set of eight Surrey Cycle Guides which have been developed in conjunction with local cycle groups. Martin Taplin, a member of the Guildford Cycle Group, has kindly offered his knowledge and expertise about the people to contact for assistance.

My thanks go to the Holmbury St Mary cyclists who have resolutely followed me whilst I have researched some of the routes and pubs, and who, together with the Holmbury walkers, have been most supportive during the writing of this guide.

Lastly, my thanks to my family and friends who have listened and made helpful suggestions. James, my son the photographer, has driven many a mile to complete his task and has shown remarkable forbearance in making various adjustments to my bicycle to enable me to cycle every yard in the book!

1

# Milford, Elstead and Thursley

## *14½ or 17 miles*

The ride starts at Secretts farm shop, crosses the River Wey and skirts the Peper Harow estate before passing through the Thursley National Nature Reserve. This is an area of lowland heath, mire and woodland where dragonflies, butterflies and even lizards can be found. Relax with a drink at Elstead Mill, enjoy the tranquil setting of the lake-side houses at Milhanger and Enton and perhaps visit the Three Horseshoes at Thursley, the village-owned pub.

**Maps:** OS Landranger 186 Aldershot and Guildford or OS Explorer 145 Guildford and Farnham (GR SU948423).

**Starting point:** Secretts at Hurst Farm, Chapel Lane, Milford have agreed that users of this book may park in their farm shop car park. From the A3 go to Milford traffic lights and driving in the Godalming direction for ¼ mile, turn sharply left into Chapel Lane and right into Secretts.

**By train:** Milford station is on the route.

**Refreshments:** The Millstream at Elstead, the Three Horseshoes at Thursley and Eliza's at Secretts. The Garden Centre at Secretts, close by on the Godalming road, also offers self-service refreshments.

**The route:** A varied ride, with a mixture of quiet roads and off-road riding on common land and tracks. Part of the ride is relatively flat, whilst the rest has hills with some good downhill runs. Provided you ride in the suggested direction there is a feeling that you have ridden more downhill than up!

To shorten the ride to 14½ miles, omit the detour to Elstead in paragraph 4.

**Turn R** at the entrance to Secretts into Chapel Lane. Go through the barrier posts at the end and **turn R** into Eashing Lane. In less than a mile **turn L** down the steep slope to cross the River Wey at attractive Eashing Bridges. **Turn R** just before the A3 and climb the track to use the bridge.

Go through a gate and **bear R**, to follow the bridle path as it crosses a field and later bends sharply **R** at another gate. Ride to Elstead Road following the woodland path. **Turn L** and ride past the grounds of Peper Harow, down the hill and over the River Wey at Somerset Bridge.

**Turn L** onto the B3001 and, after a few yards, **turn R** into a bridleway over a surfaced road past grassland and pines. In ½ mile the track splits into five

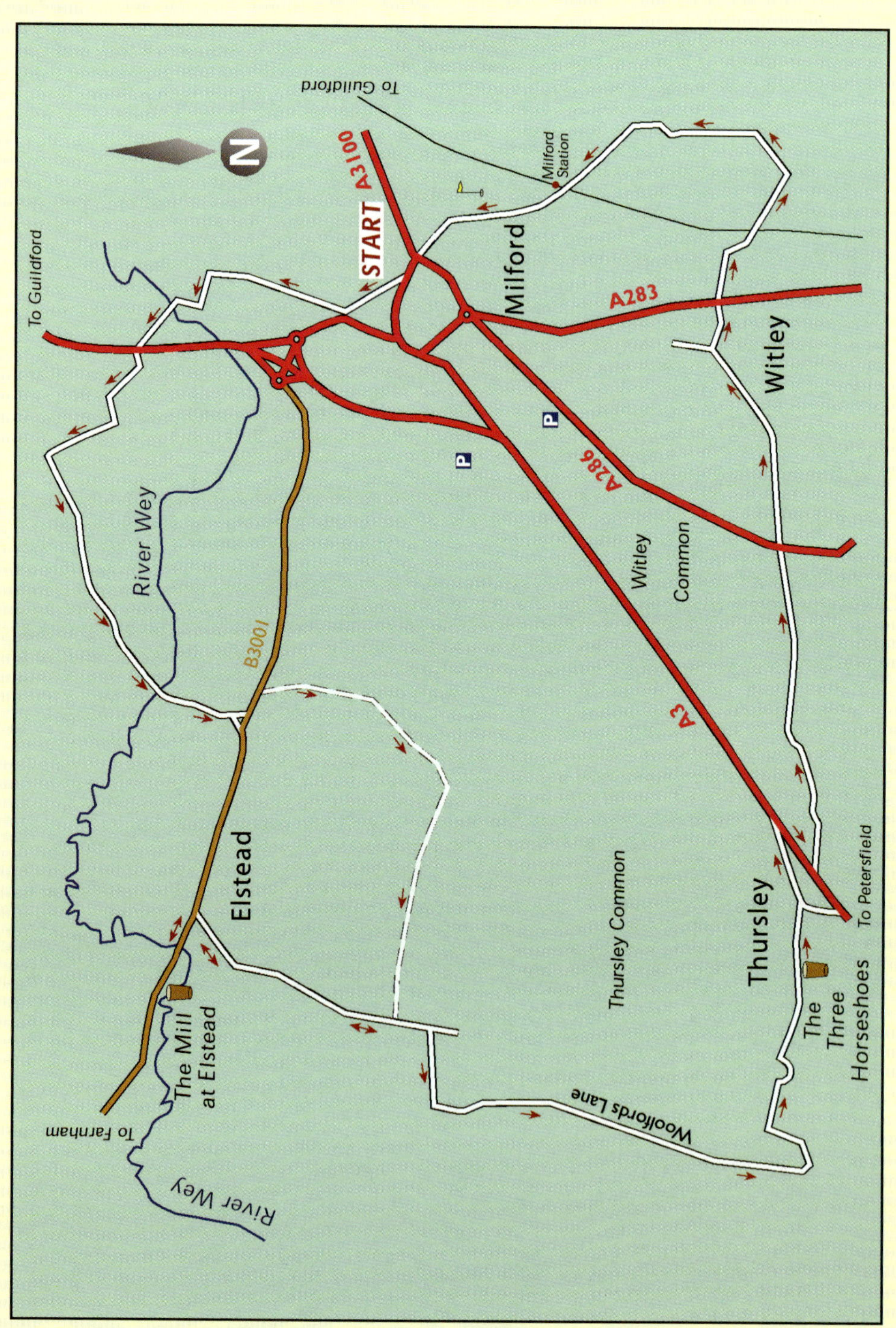
N
To Guildford
To Guildford
START
A3100
Milford Station
Milford
A283
Witley
A286
P
P
Witley Common
A3
Thursley
To Petersfield
The Three Horseshoes
Thursley Common
Woolfords Lane
River Wey
B3001
Elstead
The Mill at Elstead
To Farnham
River Wey

*The attractive Mill at Elstead*

ways. **Turn R** on the wide main track over the Defence Department's managed access land and cycle over attractive heathland for 1½ miles to the Thursley road.

For Elstead Mill, make a detour to Elstead by **turning R** and riding for 1 mile to the village. **Turn L** and the mill is about ¼ mile on the left. Have a leisurely drink or a steaming cup of coffee by the millstream, a delight on a sunny day. Retrace the route and return to the end of paragraph 3 above.

Continue the route by **turning L** down the Thursley road for ⅕ mile. **Turn R** into Woolfords Lane which you follow for 2 miles. In detail: **turn sharply L** past houses and then up a rising track, named Houndown Bottom. A short, sharp descent is a signal to bend **L** before rising to join Thursley Lane.

**Turn L** and then shortly **turn R** into Dye House Road. A good run downhill is followed by a climb up to the cricket ground at Thursley where you could rest on the seat under the oak tree. Soon the Three Horseshoes, an independent pub run by the village, is on the right.

Ride on down the hill towards the A3, then **turn R** over the bridge, SP Portsmouth. **Turn R** at the T-junction and, just before reaching the south carriageway, **turn L** into a bridleway. Ride down into Milhanger where you can enjoy the lake and attractive houses. Climb up the short hill the other side of French Lane.

**Turn L** and in a few yards **turn R** into a narrow bridleway. Negotiate the downhill path through trees and emerge at an open area by Lake Cottages. Go on to **turn R** at bridleway crossways before climbing the gently rising track for nearly ¾ mile.

*The River Wey upstream of Eashing bridge*

**Turn R** into Lea Coach Road. Ride to the crossroads and cross the A286 into Roke Lane. Glide down the hill towards Witley but **fork R** at the bottom into Roke Lane. NB: the street becomes one-way for approaching traffic.

Cross over the A283. On the corner there is an interesting specialist cane shop which sells baskets and many other cane creations. Go into Mill Lane and follow the bridleway down to Enton Mill Farm where there are more lakes. Ride under the bridge and up the track to a T-junction where you **bend R**.

**Turn L** into Water Lane and ride down the hill. At the T-junction **turn L** into Station Lane and follow the road over the level crossing at Milford station and on to Milford village, less than a mile away. **Turn R** by the shops and take the first exit, **L**, at the mini-roundabout. Shortly **turn R** to return to Chapel Lane and Secretts.

## THE NATIONAL NATURE RESERVE AT THURSLEY

Look out for dragonfly and damselfly, lizards and the rare purple emperor butterfly. Curlews regularly breed here and notable birds are woodlark, nightjar and owls, whilst the great grey shrike is a winter visitor. The River Wey appears in various guises throughout the ride and this supports a surprisingly diverse number of invertebrate species.

## THURSLEY

The village had agriculture at its core in Saxon times whilst in the 15th and 16th centuries two Thursley families became known for their cloth making. In the 17th century the iron industry was predominant as Thursley provided the Navy with cannon and shot. Two centuries later it became known for its silk weaving and there are tales of the raw silk and whiskey having been smuggled in from France.

Thursley was always affected by its proximity to the Portsmouth road. In 1767 the road was made into a turnpike and this meant that it became well used by stagecoaches and the attendant highwaymen and other villains. It was even alleged that the clergy of Thursley had been known to hold up a stagecoach in order to augment church funds. *Broomsquire*, a book by Baring-Gould, is based upon a notorious Thursley murder. In 1786 a sailor set out from the Red Lion accompanied by three men who robbed and killed him on Hindhead and threw his body into the Devil's Punch Bowl. The robbers were caught selling the sailor's clothing near Petersfield and were hanged the following year on Gibbet Hill, with chains made by the Thursley blacksmith. As a warning to other felons their bodies were left there until the gibbet blew down three years later.

# 2

# Puttenham Common, Alice Holt and Tilford

### *22 miles*

This ride starts in the south-western corner of the county, well within the Surrey Hills area, but has an excursion into cycle-friendly Alice Holt Forest in Hampshire. The countryside embraces heathland dotted with pines, woodland and stretches of waterscape such as Frensham Little Pond, a renowned beauty spot, and the Tarn at Lower Puttenham Common. The north and south branches of the River Wey meander through the area offering a feeling of tranquillity and timelessness. Waverley Abbey ruins lie at a beautiful site on the river, and bridges over the Wey are crossed at Dockenfield and Tilford.

**Maps:** OS Landranger 186 Aldershot and Guildford, OS Explorer 145 Guildford and Farnham (GR SU920461).

**Starting point:** The upper car park on Puttenham Common. From the B3001, Milford to Elstead road, turn first right after passing through Elstead. In 1¼ miles continue over the crossroads to pass the Tarn on your left. The car park is about ¾ mile further, on the left-hand side.

**By train:** Farnham station is about 1¼ miles from the route.

**Refreshments:** There is the Good Intent at Puttenham, and Manor Farm Craft Centre at Seale for teas and light lunches (closed on Mondays), whilst the Cherry Tree is at Rowledge and you'll find a snack bar and picnic tables at Alice Holt Forest. There are also the Blue Bell gastro pub at Dockenfield, the Donkey at Charleshill and the Barley Mow in Tilford. The Bridge in Millbridge also offers teas.

**The route:** The route is a mixture of quiet lanes with some short distances on slightly busier roads. There is some easy off-road riding in Alice Holt Forest, as well as a mile near Dockenfield. There are some ups and downs but these are interspersed with flatter sections.

**Turn L** out of the car park and cycle 1½ miles into Puttenham. There is a large white house, Puttenham Priory, to your right which dates back to the 13th century, and a large pig farm to your left. **Turn L** in Puttenham village to cycle parallel to the Hog's Back on the NCN22. This is a quiet, pastoral lane which climbs towards Seale church. Soon Manor Farm Craft Centre is to your right with a variety of tempting craft shops.

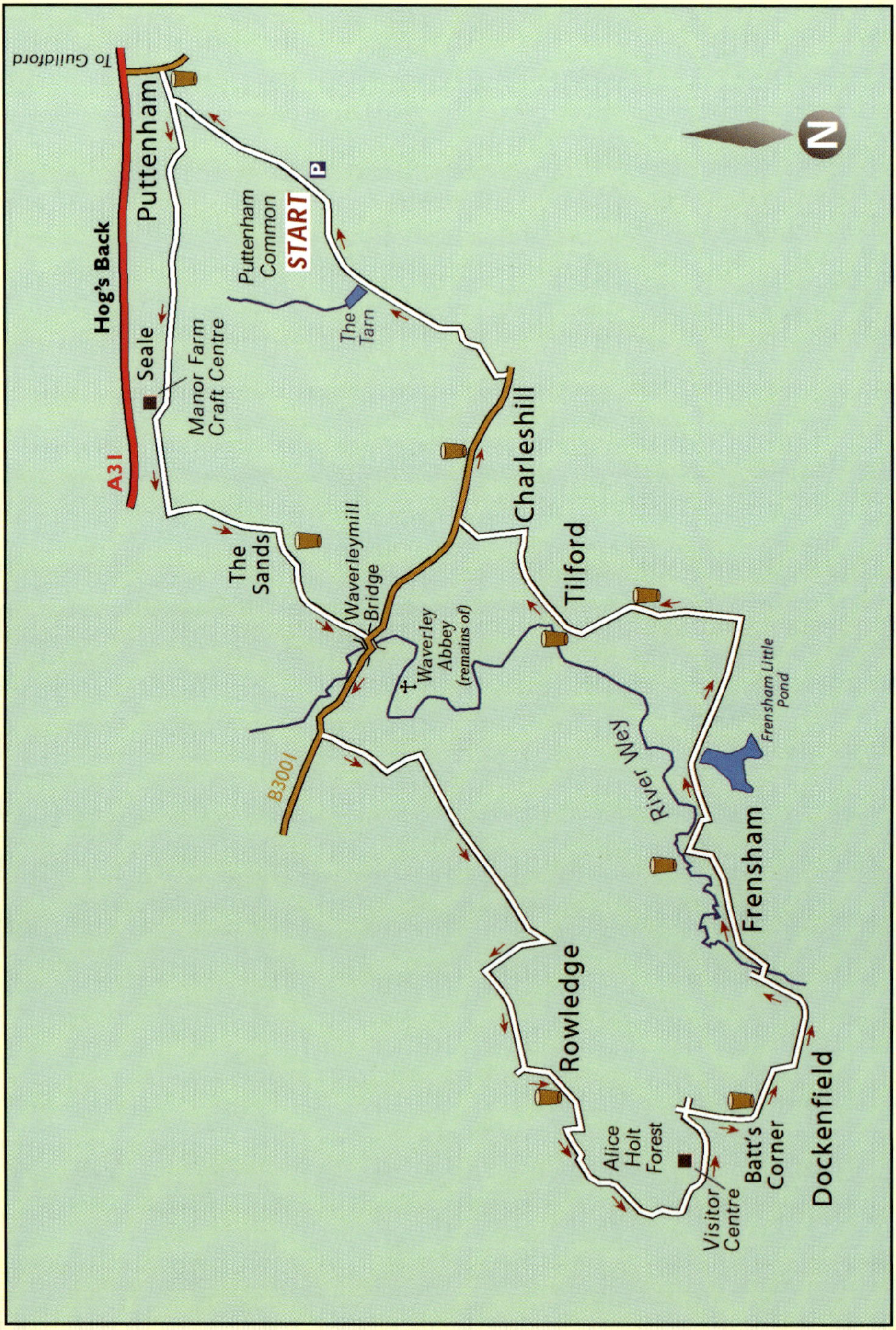

# 2 Puttenham Common, Alice Holt and Tilford

*Frensham Little Pond*

**Bear L** to continue on the NCN22 for ⅔ mile. **Turn L** into Binton Lane. Go ahead at The Sands crossroads unless you wish to patronize the Barley Mow to your left. Climb Botany Hill and run downwards to cross into Camp Hill at off-set crossroads. **Turn R** onto the B3001 and, on your left, you can go through the gate to wander by the river to the ruins of the first Cistercian monastery in the country, Waverley Abbey.

Ride for ¾ mile on the B3001 then **turn L** into Monk's Walk. At the crossroads **turn L**. Go down the hill and in ⅓ mile **turn R** into Dene Lane, a bridleway. Steer a straight course for over 1½ miles, crossing roads and riding on both hard surfaces and tracks. (From Dene Lane to Latchford the crossing is off-set, so **turn L** and then **R**).

**Turn R** to climb Gardener's Hill at the T-junction at Edgeborough. **Turn L** in ⅔ mile, at the crossroads, into Boundstone Road. Follow the major road for over a mile to Rowledge village. **Turn R** and immediately **L**, and the Cherry Tree pub is soon on your right.

Cross over into Church Lane and ride onto the narrow path to Alice Holt Forest. **Turn R** at the five-way crosspaths to bend left along the ridge. Take the detour from marker post 22 to beautiful Lodge pond. The path returns to the main track, descends and curves left. Go through the barrier and **turn second L** to the visitor centre where information and snacks are available.

Take the path opposite the bicycle rentals, SP 'Family Bike Route'. Ride for nearly ¾ mile, crossing a main track. Watch for a small white 'Esso 2' marker stone, where you **turn R** along a narrow path leading to Boundary Road.

**Turn R** and climb the hill to Batt's Corner and the Blue Bell pub. **Turn L** onto the track alongside the Blue Bell garden. Keep ahead and shortly there is

*The 14th-century church at Frensham*

a clearing on the right with a seat, a peaceful spot, which provides the ideal setting for a picnic. Follow the track/road down to the Street at Dockenfield. **Turn L** and, passing Dockenfield Farm, ride for over ¾ mile to **turn R** over the River Wey and pool into Mill Lane. This attractive lane leads past the village of Frensham with the church of St Mary the Virgin, dating back to the 14th century.

**Turn L** onto the A287 to sail down the hill, but soon **turn first R** into Priory Lane unless you decide to visit the delightful Bridge for tea in Millbridge. Priory Lane passes close to Frensham Little Pond, where you can enjoy the shimmering water and tiny beach. Go over the ford and ride a mile along the lane past nurseries to the Tilford road. **Turn L** at the T-junction and Tilford, with its triangular cricket green and pub, is just over a mile away.

**Turn R** across the bridge and soon **turn R** into Whitmead Lane. Follow the lane as it turns sharply left and rises to the T-junction. **Turn R** onto the B3001 and ride for 1⅕ miles past the Donkey pub to **turn second L** into Fulbrook Lane. In 1¼ miles there are crossroads by the Tarn. Go straight over and, on your left, there is a good view of the lake from the small causeway bridge, separated from Cuttmill Pond to your right. Climb steadily for ¾ mile, back to the car park.

## ALICE HOLT FOREST

Alice Holt, run by the Forestry Commission, is known for its scientific research into the effects of forests upon climate change mitigation and also for its woodland management for the benefit of wildlife. It has gradually developed walking and cycling paths and a play area in its 850 hectares, making it a popular area for recreation. Once a great hunting forest, Alice Holt supplied the royal court with venison from red and fallow deer until they were moved to Windsor in the 18th century. These have been replaced by roe and muntjac deer. Many species of wildlife can be observed, including bats, amphibians and reptiles, but of particular note is the elusive purple emperor butterfly, the emblem of this forest.

## WAVERLEY ABBEY

The Cistercian Order, whose foundation was in Citeaux, Burgundy, founded Waverley Abbey in 1128. The Order, which was considered to be both ascetic and austere, sought houses in isolated and remote valleys where the land could be worked by lay brothers. The 60-acre Waverley site was chosen and the community thrived and expanded so that Waverley became mother house to five more houses, the second being Tintern in Wales. It later offered shelter to passing pilgrims and an infirmary for the sick, until the dissolution of the monasteries in 1536. The path to the abbey ruins past Waverley House is through meadows by the meandering River Wey and over a fine three-arched bridge built by the monks.

## 3

# Chiddingfold, Haslemere and Blackdown

### *16 or 14 miles*

This is a circuit on quiet lanes which crosses into West Sussex for a few miles, to run just south of the Surrey boundary. It stretches from Chiddingfold, with its 14th-century Crown Inn, to Haslemere, a bustling town with a wide High Street, used in Victorian times as a cattle market. Climb towards Blackdown whose summit, at 919 ft, is the highest in Sussex. You will reach 777 ft on the road but you could leave your bike and climb to the very top. Two miles of winding descent through woodland follows, with the highlight of the farm shop at Lower Roundhurst, an organic farm with a pedigree herd of Sussex cattle. Ride back through Shillinglee to return to Chiddingfold, where you can relax and have tea and delicious cakes at the Green Room.

**Maps:** OS Landranger 186 Aldershot and Guildford, OS Explorer 133 Haslemere and Petersfield (GR SU961354).

**Starting point:** The Crown Inn at Chiddingfold, or park in the road beside the Green. From Guildford take the A3 towards Portsmouth and then the exit towards Milford. Take the A283, following the signs towards Petworth. When you reach the Green at Chiddingfold, the Crown is on your left opposite the church.

**By train:** Haslemere station is about ½ mile from the route. **Turn L** out of the station onto the B2131. Follow the route from paragraph 2 by turning right to climb College Hill.

**Refreshments:** Haslemere is well supplied with inns and coffee shops. There is Darnley's Café, or Russells opposite, halfway down the High Street, both of which serve coffees, teas and light lunches. Alternatively try Wetherspoon's Swan Inn, or the White Horse opposite, both at the bottom of the High Street. Lower Roundhurst Farm, beyond Blackdown, is an interesting place with a variety of food and gifts for sale. At the beginning, or end, of the ride there are the historic Crown Inn and Green Room.

**The route:** Most of the route is on quiet lanes and roads with several miles on the Surrey Cycle Way. There are no off-road tracks or paths. Haslemere High Street is busy but it is a short section where you can push your bike. There are some hills to negotiate but, to compensate, there is a wonderful run down from Blackdown, with just one or two switchbacks.
**To shorten the route to 14 miles:** Nearly ¾ mile past the main Blackdown car park, turn left along Jay's Lane. At the bottom, **turn L** into Jobson's Lane and ride to Gospel Green. Go to paragraph 4. You will, however, miss Lower Roundhurst Farm.

*Chiddingfold*

Cross over to St Mary's church and ride into Coxcombe Lane. **Turn first L**, go up the hill and after 1¼ miles **turn L** to follow the Surrey Cycle Way for a further 4 miles. The SCW is well signposted by brown signs guiding you along the wooded lanes towards Grayswood. Ride up Clammer Hill and, still following the signs, go on to the T-junction with the A286.

**Turn L** into Haslemere High Street. Look out for Darnley's café, or Russells opposite, where you can choose to sit and relax at a table on either of the forecourts, or go to the southern end of the High Street for the Swan Inn and the White Horse. From the bottom of the High Street you use residential roads around the town to avoid the busy B2131. You will find the route if you keep climbing toward Blackdown! In detail: from the bottom of the High Street bear **R** and then go immediately **L** to climb up College Hill. **Turn L** at the top into Hill Road and then first **R** into Old Haslemere Road. **Turn L** into Scotland Lane and ride for ¼ mile passing the recreation ground. At the five-way junction **turn R** into The Chase and shortly **L** into Tennyson's Lane, signposted 'Blackdown'.

Climb gradually upwards through shady woodland into National Trust land and the car parks at Blackdown. Here you may wish to lock your bike and climb to the top of Blackdown hill on foot to enjoy the views over the wooded Weald.

From the car parks descend along the lane and on your left, in a mile, look out for Lower Roundhurst Farm where you can stop and enjoy refreshments whilst looking at the organic produce. They even offer breakfast! In just over a mile at the base of the hill, **turn L** at the T-junction and ride downwards along attractive Jobson's Lane towards Gospel Green.

At Gospel Green **turn R** and go on to cross the A283 towards Shillinglee. In 1½ miles **turn L** at Shillinglee Home Farm. **Turn L** again at the T-junction and cycle 2 miles back to Chiddingfold.

## BLACKDOWN

Blackdown, at 919 ft, is the highest hill in Sussex and lies within the South Downs National Park. Owned by the National Trust, it is an area popular with walkers for its wild beauty and superb views to

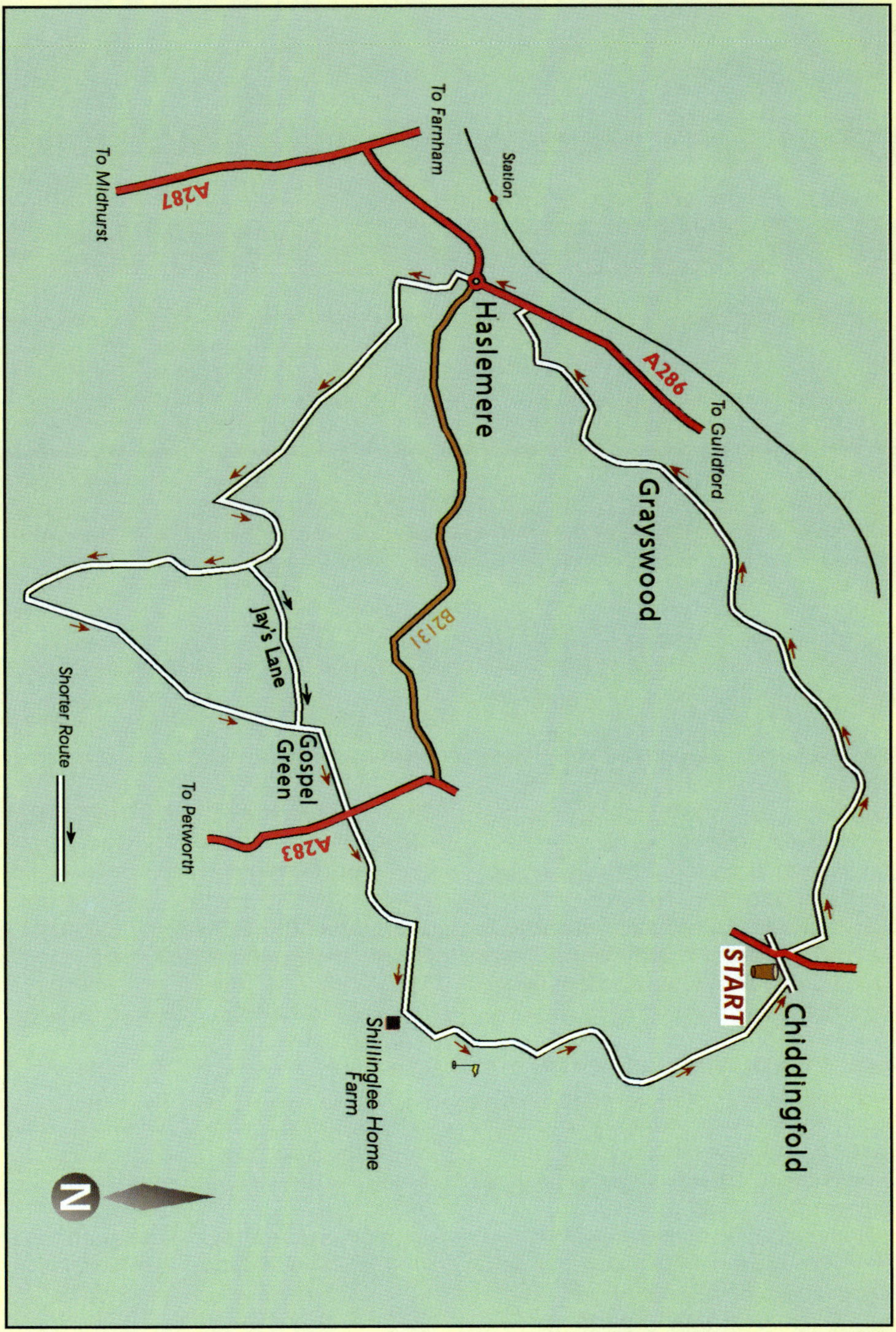

To Midhurst
A287
To Farnham
Station
Haslemere
A286
To Guildford
Grayswood
B2131
Jay's Lane
Gospel Green
Shorter Route
To Petworth
A283
START
Chiddingfold
Shillinglee Home Farm
N

*The town of Haslemere*

the South Downs. In 1869, recognizing the tranquillity of the area, the poet Alfred Lord Tennyson built his house, Aldworth, on this greensand ridge overlooking the Weald. Tennyson's Lane, named after the poet, runs along the northern slopes of the hill and is on the cycle route. Sadly the hill has a darker moment in its history. There was an air crash in November 1967 when a Caravelle passenger plane owned by Iberia, bound from Malaga to Heathrow, crashed into the southern side of the hillside in misty conditions.

## LOWER ROUNDHURST FARM

This is an organic farm whose philosophy is to produce well cared for and beautiful animals in an unspoilt and healthy environment. There is a herd of pedigree Sussex cattle as well as sheep and pigs and these can be seen on open days. A shop sells meat from the farm, free-range organic eggs, locally-produced vegetables, pots of home-made jams, pickles and sauces, as well as gift shop items. The café is open six days a week, Mondays excepted, and serves everything from a cappucino to all-day breakfasts, lunches and teas.

## THE CROWN INN, CHIDDINGFOLD

The Crown is a most attractive half-timbered building and dates back at least as far as the 14th century. It may go back even further to 1285, when it is thought that there was a guest house upon the site used by Cistercian monks making their way to Waverley Abbey, as they travelled between Winchester and Canterbury. There are various historic rooms inside, as well as a modern extension. The church of St Mary is across the road from the Crown. The window at the west end is said to be made up of 427 fragments of glass which were dug up near the old glass furnaces in Chiddingfold which once provided glass for the royal chapels, including St George's at Windsor.

# 4

# Dunsfold, Hambledon and Hascombe

*19½ miles*

This route starts in the pretty village of Dunsfold and then goes to Vann Lane where stands Vann house and the internationally renowned Gertrude Jekyll water garden. Pause at Hambledon post office for a drink overlooking the cricket green. Then cycle over Hambledon Common, pass tranquil Sweetwater Lake and ride on to Enton and Milford. At Secretts you can indulge at Eliza's café or enjoy the sights and aromas in the deli. Follow the River Wey towpath at Godalming before climbing up to Munstead and past the National Trust's much admired Winkworth Arboretum. There is still the White Horse at Hascombe and the 13th-century church of St Mary and All Saints at Dunsfold, to experience on your return.

**Maps:** OS Landranger 186 Aldershot and Guildford, OS Explorers 134 Crawley and Horsham, 145 Guildford and Farnham and 133 Haslemere and Petersfield (GR TQ006361).

**Starting point:** The car park at Dunsfold. From the B2130 Godalming to Cranleigh road take the turning towards Dunsfold. In a mile there is a gravelled parking area on the right, just before reaching the Sun pub.

**By train:** Godalming and Milford stations are on the route.

**Refreshments:** The Sun at Dunsfold, the village shop at Hambledon which offers excellent snacks, Eliza's tea room and Secretts Garden Centre at Milford, Hector's riverside café opposite Catteshall Lock, the café at Winkworth Arboretum and the White Horse at Hascombe.

**The route:** There are mainly quiet lanes with 3 miles on bridleways and river towpath and 3 on the busier, but downward sloping B2130. Climbs over the folds of the hills are relatively short. Pushing may be necessary on sandy sections in dry weather conditions, but there is an alternative road option through Godalming, shown on the map.

**Turn R** out of the car park and ride past the Sun pub in the direction of Chiddingfold for nearly 2 miles. Watch for a **R turn** into White Beech Lane. In ¾ mile **turn R** at the T-junction to follow quiet Vann Lane towards Hambledon. Eventually you reach the cricket green and the amazing Hambledon village shop where you may decide to take a break at one of the outdoor tables. Perhaps sip a drink and choose from their range of cakes and croissants.

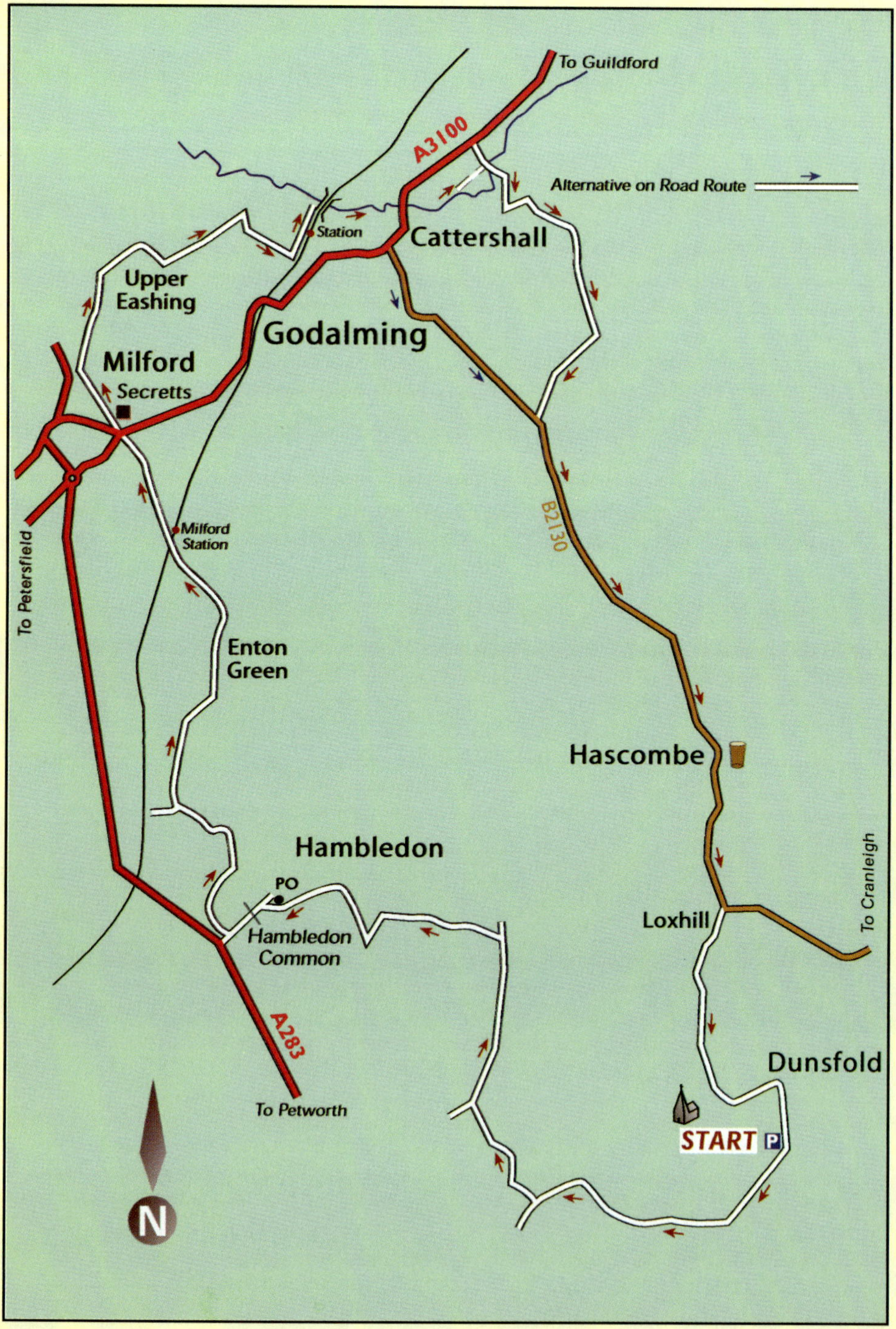

# 4 Dunsfold, Hambledon and Hascombe

To Guildford
A3100
Alternative on Road Route
Station
Cattershall
Upper Eashing
Godalming
Milford
Secretts
Milford Station
To Petersfield
B2130
Enton Green
Hascombe
Hambledon
PO
Hambledon Common
To Cranleigh
Loxhill
A283
Dunsfold
To Petworth
START
P
N

*Catteshall lock on the River Wey*

**Turn L** at the T-junction, SP Milford. Just before reaching the A283 **turn R** into Wormley Lane and in ¼ mile, **R** onto the bridleway by Hambledon Place across Hambledon Common. In ½ mile, at a crossways, **fork half L** along a narrow bridleway where you may need to push for a short distance. Join a wide driveway and in ½ mile reach Sweetwater Pond. **Turn R** at a T-junction into Water Lane. Climb the hill and enjoy the view opposite Enton Hall.

Sail downhill along the tree-lined lane for 1¼ miles to Enton Green. **Turn L** at the T-junction, go over the level crossing at Milford station and ride to the T-junction at Milford. **Turn R** and take the first exit onto the A3100 at the mini-roundabout. In a few yards **turn R** into Chapel Lane and Secretts is on your right. Viewing the deli, where there is a veritable Aladdin's cave of goodies, the greengrocery and Eliza's café, makes for a most enjoyable break. A faster cafeteria service is available at Secretts Garden Centre, a less than ½ mile detour towards Godalming.

Ride to the end of Chapel Lane and **turn R** through the posts into Eashing Lane. Climb the hill and, after a sharp right-hand bend **turn L** into Halfway Lane, passing Fitzpatrickreferrals, a renowned small animal orthopaedics centre. Follow the lane to a narrow bridleway and descend through woods before riding beside the railway at Godalming.

**Turn R** under the railway bridge and

soon **L** into Village Way, a narrow alleyway. You should push your bike here and in the Phillips Memorial Park across the road, to follow the riverside walk. At Godalming library **turn L** and after the bridge **R** into the church entrance to the River Wey towpath and cycle ½ mile to Catteshall lock.

**Turn R** onto Catteshall Road. Hector's café is down the steps on the left on the far side of the river. In ⅓ mile from the lock go round the right-hand bend.

**Turn sharply L** into Catteshall Lane. Keep straight ahead and **turn R** in front of a timbered white cottage, taking the bridleway for 1 mile past Springfield Farm. **Turn R** onto the road at the top and in ⅓ mile, by the water tower, **turn half L** onto a bridleway. Ride ahead for ⅓ mile, crossing a lane, to the B2130, where you **turn L**.

Ride for about ¾ mile to pass the National Trust's Winkworth Arboretum. In a further 1½ miles you could visit the White Horse, St Peter's church and the attractive green at Hascombe. Ride for nearly a mile to Loxhill and **turn second R** into Hookhouse Road. In a mile consider a **R turn** into Church Green to visit the 13th-century church of St Mary and All Saints, one of the highlights of Dunsfold. Back on the lane, climb the short hill to the village, **turn R** at the T-junction and the car park is on your right.

## GODALMING

Godalming is a small country town nestling in a steep and narrow valley on the banks of the River Wey. When the river is high it overflows into the Lamas Lands, or watermeadows, a site of nature conservation. The Phillips Memorial Gardens by the river walk were designed in memory of John George Phillips, Chief Wireless Telegraphist on the *Titanic*, who remained at his post as she sank. The gardens inside and around the cloister were designed by Gertrude Jekyll, another local resident. Having had a flourishing cloth industry from the 13th century and later being known for its knitwear, stockings and tanneries, Godalming is also famous for being the first town in the world to have street lights powered by electricity. In 1881 a generator at the leather mill was found to provide sufficient power for the town gas supply to be disconnected.

In 1726 Mary Tofts, a town resident, claimed to have given birth to rabbits! She persuaded some eminent physicians, such as Nathaniel St André, surgeon to the Royal Household of George I, that this had occurred and was taken to London for further investigations. As would be expected, it was eventually found to be a hoax. She was charged and imprisoned but soon released.

## WINKWORTH ARBORETUM

A beautiful place to visit at any time, in spring the slopes are full of flowering plants and shrubs such as bluebells, azaleas and magnolia, whilst in autumn there are spectacular displays of vibrant leaf colour. There are views over to the North Downs and the greensand ridge and a tranquil lake and wetland area lie at the base of the slopes. Many of the trees were planted in the 1930s by Dr Wilfred Fox who was passionate about trees and saw great potential in the unspoiled sloping landscape. Although he was an amateur, he became an authority on his subject and was awarded the Victoria Medal of Honour for his work. The National Trust acquired the land in 1952.

5

# Puttenham Common, Guildford and Christmas Pie

## *22 miles*

This ride describes an oblong around the Hog's Back, starting at the tranquil Tarn, one of six large ponds on Puttenham Common. Visit Watts Gallery and tea room, the picturesque villages of Puttenham and Compton, and view Guildford Cathedral from the high trackway on the Downs. Enjoy the relaxed atmosphere of the river from the Wey towpath before crossing the University campus to the intriguingly-named Christmas Pie trail which meanders from Guildford to Runfold. Here you can enjoy the highlight of Packhouse Antiques with its exotic emporium and the Fig Leaf café.

**Maps:** OS Landranger 186 Aldershot and Guildford, OS Explorer 145 Guildford and Farnham (GR SU911455).

**Starting point:** The car park at the Tarn, Puttenham. Turn south from the Hog's Back for ¼ mile on the B3000 and turn left towards Puttenham village. Soon turn left past the church in the direction of Elstead. Drive for just over 2 miles and the Tarn car park is on your right by crossroads.

**By train:** Guildford station.

**Refreshments:** Watts Gallery at Compton has a teashop and the YMCA's river-view restaurant at Guildford. The Fig Leaf is at Packhouse Antiques at Runfold, the Barley Mow is at The Sands and the Cyder House Inn is in Shackleford.

**The route:** North of the Hog's Back on the Christmas Pie Trail the route is comparatively flat whereas to the south there are some climbs up to the Hog's Back. About two-thirds is on a variety of easy off-road surfaces and much of the rest is on quiet roads. Check your brakes for the steep descent into Guildford.

From the Tarn car park, pedal straight on for 2 miles to the village of Shackleford. Aldro School is to your right as you enter this delightful village of sandstone and mature brick houses. **Turn L** for the route, or **turn R** and **fork R** for the Cyder House. Climb towards Puttenham and the Hog's Back with a large pig farm to your right.

Unless you intend to explore Puttenham, cross the B3000, **turn L** on the pavement and soon **turn R** onto the NCN22, which you follow into Guildford. The detail is in paragraph 2, or skip straight to paragraph 3.

In detail: cycle for 1½ miles on the track past the golf course and go under

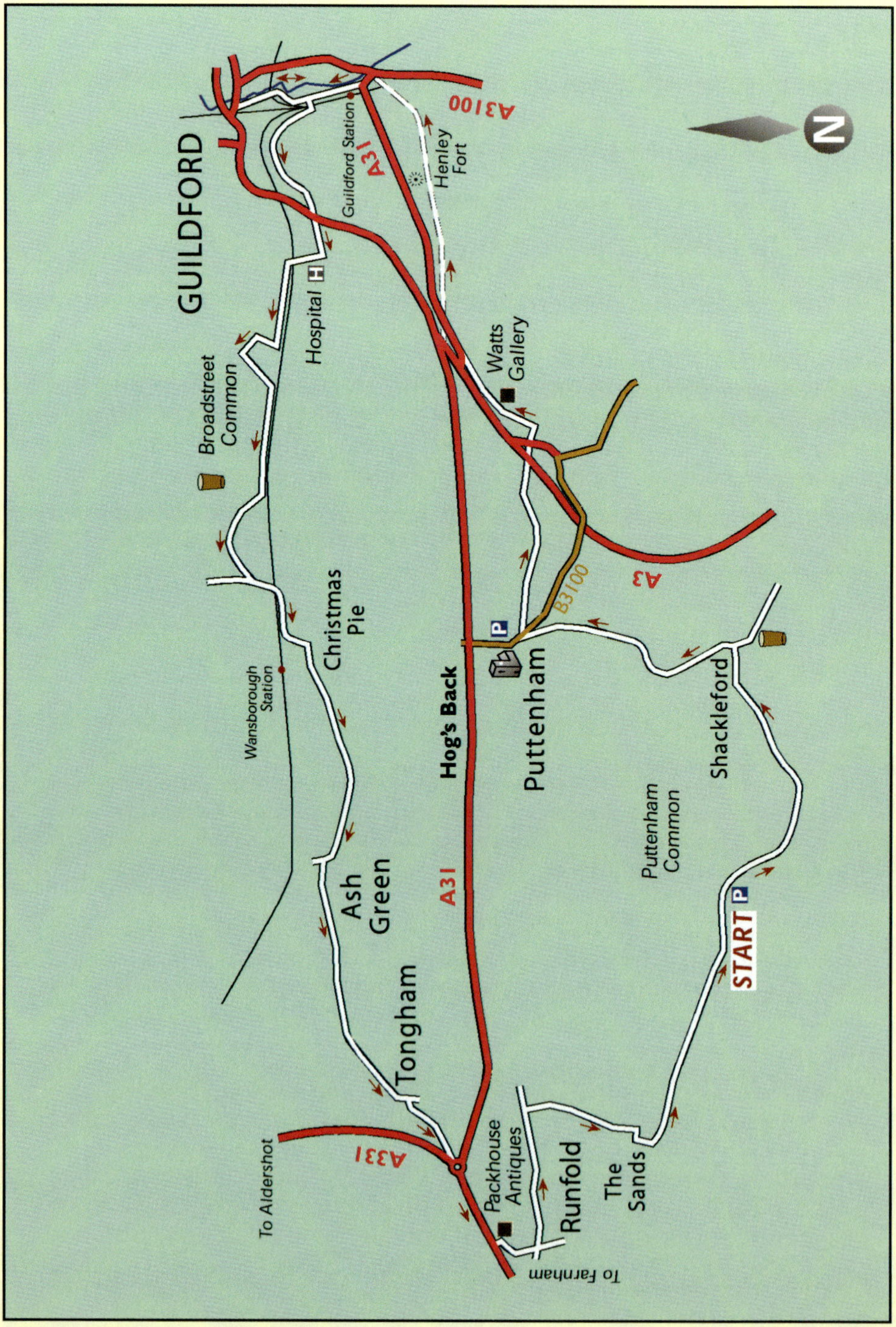

# 5 Puttenham Common, Guildford and Christmas Pie

*The surfaced towpath on the way to Dapdune Wharf*

the A3. **Turn L** into Down Lane, and the Watts Gallery gift and tea shop is on your right. Climb the lane and **turn R** by the A3. Yards before the next T-junction cross to the right-hand wall and **turn R** onto the trackway for 1¾ miles. Pause to see long views to the left to Canary Wharf and pass Henley Fort, the outdoor centre, before making the steep descent into Guildford.

Cross towards St Nicholas' church and **turn L** beside the river for 1 mile, keeping the river on your right. Soon watch for the YMCA, climb the steps and enjoy the refreshments, high above the river. Pass Dapdune Wharf on your right and, at the railway bridge, **turn sharply L** into busy Walnut Tree Close for ¼ mile. **Turn R**, immediately after Addison's Glass, onto a narrow road with a signboard to Jewson's entrance. Go under the railway and up to the University of Surrey.

**Turn R** and follow the road past the fountain and car parks. **Turn R** onto the shared pathway at the pedestrian lights just after the mini-roundabout, near the university entrance. You can divert to visit Guildford Cathedral by going to the entrance, by the stag, and turning left up to the top of Stag Hill.

Back on the route, remain on the shared pathways as far as Southway. In detail: keep ahead on the path for ½ mile, keeping to the route with the metal barriers and the two underpasses. At the first roundabout near Tesco, cross to go straight ahead, still on the pathways. **Turn R** at the next roundabout into Egerton Road, remaining on the shared way opposite the Royal Surrey County Hospital. Go over the railway and take the first exit at the roundabout into Southway and cycle for ¼ mile.

*The Tarn, at the start of the ride*

**Turn L** into Applegarth Avenue for ½ mile and, just before Hunt's Close, **turn L** onto a pathway between two houses, signed as the Christmas Pie Trail. At the gate **turn L** onto the narrow pathway across Broadstreet Common. Look for the Christmas Pie cycle trail symbol, a Christmas pudding

encircled by a green ring. You should now be able to follow the signs for the next 7 miles towards Runfold. Skip to (*), or follow the detailed route below.

In detail: the trail opens up at Broad Street Common and the pathway is to the left of the notice-board. This is an unlikely-looking, narrow, meandering path which is a joy to ride. The path veers right towards Wood Street cricket ground. **Turn L** at a crossing of bridleways to pass through more woodland and later under the railway bridge. Bend sharply right beside the railway. **Bear L** up Flexford Lane, now **bear R**, and go straight ahead to the Christmas Pie crossroads.

Cross over into the lane which changes to rough track. When the metalled surface returns, ride for ⅓ mile and watch for Pound Farm where you **turn L** onto a public byway. Ride for over a mile, crossing a road at Ash Green. **Turn L** onto the dismantled railway line towards Tongham. At the end of the track **bear R**, go through the barrier, **bear L** and soon **turn L** to Tongham. At the mini roundabout **turn R** into a lane and perhaps see miniature Shetlands and a donkey in the fields. **Bear L** on the path to the roundabout and cross the busy A331 onto a pathway eventually leading to a quiet lane.

(*) Packhouse Antiques is ½ mile along the lane to Runfold, a huge emporium of fascinating antiques, fabrics and gifts where you can also visit the Fig Leaf café. Try sitting at the table under the wonderful fig tree! Soon take the second exit at the roundabout and **turn L** at the T-junction opposite the former Jolly Farmer, currently a Chinese restaurant. In ½ mile **fork R**, onto the NCN22.

In a further ½ mile **turn R** into Binton Lane. After the right-hand bend **turn L** to The Sands and soon **L** into Littleworth Road. After a gentle climb enjoy a mile-long run down back to the Tarn.

## GUILDFORD

Guildford is built around a gap in the North Downs carved out by the River Wey. It has a population of over 67,000 and a modern cathedral and university on Stag Hill overlooking the town. The cobbled High Street and the Guildhall clock, dating back to 1683, are the much-photographed face of Guildford but there is a considerable history and very many ancient buildings to be explored. Visit the Tourist Office in Tunsgate to collect details of, for example, the castle, now in ruins, a favourite of Henry III, and Abbots Hospital, near the top of the High Street, a group of impressive early 17th-century almshouses which still house 20 residents of Guildford.

## CHRISTMAS PIE

The hamlet of Christmas Pie is thought to have been named after a prominent family called Christmas who owned a farm in the area in the reign of Henry VIII. The name is often mentioned in Court records of the period. Pie originates from the Saxon 'pightel' meaning a small piece of arable land. There used to be a small field called Pie Field near the Christmas Pie crossroads, which has added to the speculation.

6

# Bramley, the Wey and Stoke Park

*15 miles*

A shorter ride offering an insight into the diversity of the environs of Guildford. Ride along the Downs Link, experience the locks and narrow-boats of the gently-flowing River Wey, as well as seeing Guildford at work. You will pass Surrey University with its large pond and fountain and you could take the opportunity to visit imposing Guildford Cathedral on Stag Hill, as well as the National Trust-owned Dapdune Wharf, or perhaps the large lido, for a cooling swim. Should you have a sense of déjà vu this is because 2½ miles of river towpath and university campus area are shared with route 5.

**Maps:** OS Landranger 186 Aldershot and Guildford, OS Explorer 145 Guildford and Farnham, and the free leaflet 'Cycle Guildford' available from Guildford Borough Council (GR TQ010451)

**Starting point:** The car park at the disused Bramley station on the Downs Link. From the A281 Guildford to Horsham road turn left at the mini-roundabout in Bramley. The car park is on your left just after St Catherine's school.

**By train:** Shalford and Guildford stations.

**Refreshments:** The Jolly Farmer pub at Bramley, the Snooty Fox snack bar and the Seahorse pub at Shalford. The excellent YMCA restaurant is on the river towpath in Guildford; the Row Barge is at Stoke alongside the river; and snacks are available at the National Trust's Dapdune Wharf.

**The route:** Generally an easy route with several shared pedestrian/cycle ways in urban areas where there are usually crossings for busy roads. There are steps down to the river towpath on the return. The alternative routes by the river are best ridden in slightly drier conditions.

To visit Guildford Cathedral, go to the university entrance; Stag Hill is on the left.

**Turn L** onto the Downs Link and cycle towards Guildford. Cross the A281 Guildford to Horsham road and soon a bridge across the River Wey. Shortly ride beneath a road bridge and **turn R** to pedal alongside the A248 on the shared path to Broadford Bridge.

**Either:** Cross Broadford Bridge, NCN22, soon **turn L** onto a track and then **half R** onto a path across Shalford Common past cottages. Keep straight ahead over the railway bridge and then ride the almost 1¼ miles towards Guildford on the cyclepath, past the rear entrance to the attractive Seahorse pub and

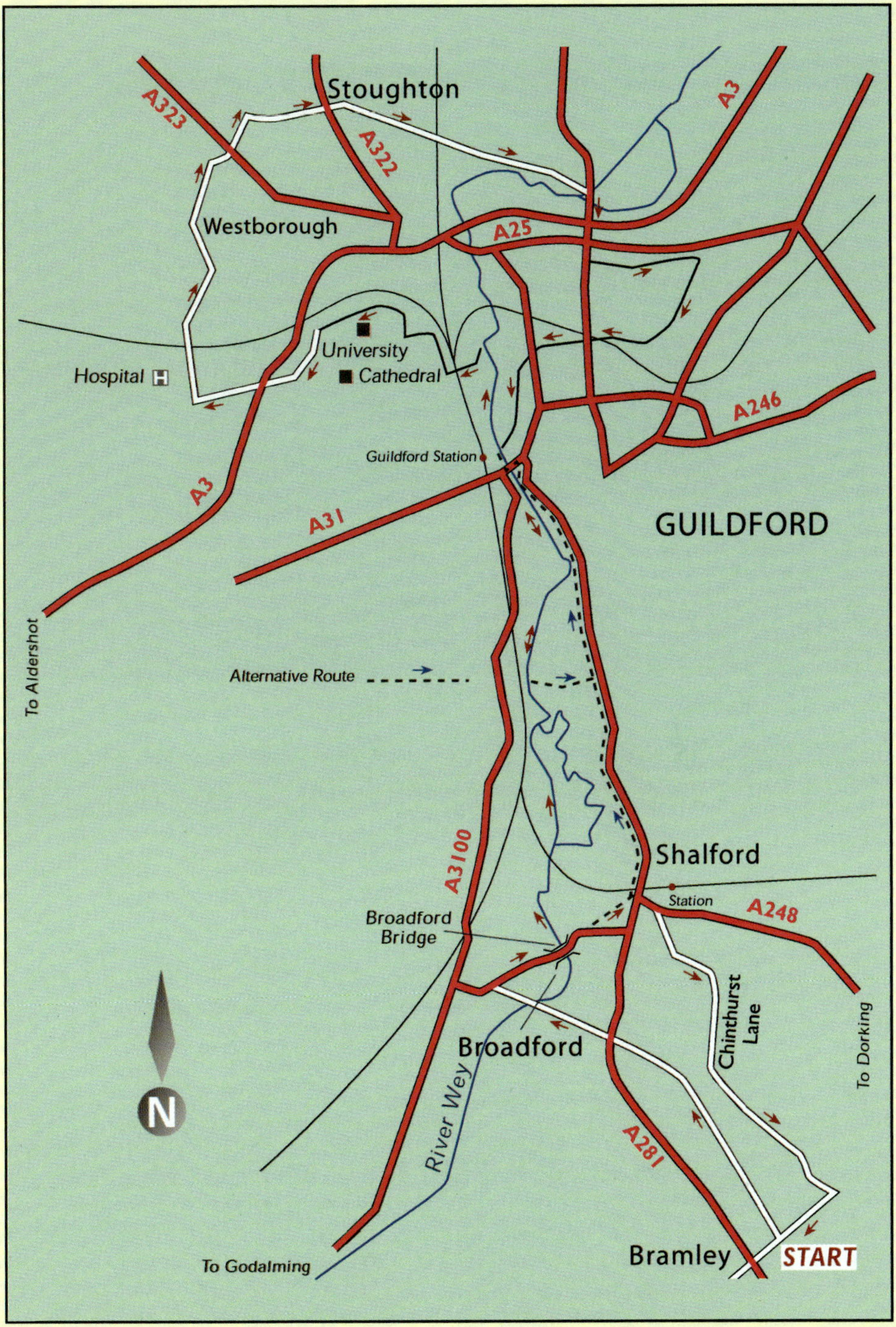

Stoughton
A323
A322
A3
Westborough
A25
University
Cathedral
Hospital H
A246
Guildford Station
A3
A31
GUILDFORD
To Aldershot
Alternative Route
A3100
Shalford
Station
A248
Broadford
Bridge
Chinthurst
Lane
N
Broadford
River Wey
To Dorking
A281
To Godalming
Bramley
START

*The Downs Link near Shalford*

through Shalford Park. At the river bridge, ride on the cycle track and **turn L** into the entrance for the Yvonne Arnaud Theatre. Here you should push your bike to the lock and across the pedestrian bridge.

**Or: turn L** from Broadford Bridge along the river towpath to ride for 1¾ miles past a lock and the ruins of St Catherine's to Guildford. Ride over the weir to the town lock by the Yvonne Arnaud Theatre. **Turn L** to cross the pedestrian bridge.

**Turn R** keeping the river on your right for 1 mile. Consider pausing at the YMCA to climb the steps and enjoy refreshments, high above the river. Pass Dapdune Wharf to your right and, at the railway bridge, **turn sharp L** into busy Walnut Tree Close for ¼ mile. **Turn R** onto a lane by a Jewson's board, passing over the railway and up to Surrey University.

**Turn R** and follow the road past the fountain, car parks and mini-roundabout towards the university entrance. At the crossing lights **turn R** into the shared pathway.

Keep ahead going through metal barriers and underpasses, keeping ahead across the road near Tesco. In ½ mile **turn R** on the shared pathway in Egerton Road, opposite the Royal Surrey County Hospital. **Turn R** to cross the railway bridge and roundabout to King's College.

Cycle up the hill on Park Barn Drive.

Keeping downhill, **turn R** at two mini-roundabouts cycling into Broad Street. Ride straight across a large roundabout into Rydes Hill. **Turn R** at Sheperd's Lane. Cross the A322 at the traffic lights and sail down Stoughton Road and over the railway bridge for over ¾ mile. At a bend in the road, by Jeans Florists, **turn R** into Riverside. Soon the Rowbarge pub is on your right by the river, a beautiful place to rest with a drink on a sunny day.

Go to the Woking road, **turn R** onto the shared pathway and go ahead to cross the A3 and the Guildford bypass using the toucan crossing and then the bridge. Cross Stoke Road to St John's church and **turn R**. Soon **turn sharp L** passing the lido and carry on up the hill. At Stoke Park **fork R** onto the shared path, soon making your way to the right onto a wider pathway sloping upwards past tennis courts.

**Turn R** into Nightingale Road. Sail down the hill and **turn L** under the railway bridge. Soon **turn R** at the Stoke pub and go to the end of Markenfield Road. Cross over Woodbridge Road into Wharf Road by the sports ground. Soon you can visit Dapdune Wharf on your right (see route 7).

Take the pedestrian walkway into William Road and make your way to the River Wey. **Turn R** into Mary Road and follow the one-way route bending right past the County Court and Bedford Road car park. Passing the

*The riverside path near Broadford Bridge*

Crown Court, soon cross to your right to the area by Old Orleans and the Odeon cinema to the river. Walk your bike up the ramp and cross the bridge. Go down the steps to the towpath, **turn R** and cycle back past the White House pub, retracing the outward journey to the town lock.

**Either:** walk your bike past the loch and towards Millbrook. **Turn R**, pushing your bike until the signs indicate a shared path past Millmead car park. Cycle into Shalford Park.
**Or:** cycle on the river towpath for over ½ mile to the bridge at St Catherine's. Cross the river to the footpath leading to Shalford Park and cross the grass to the cycle path.

Ride towards Shalford and cross the railway bridge. **Turn L** past the recycling unit to the A281 and cross over. Soon **turn R** into Chinthurst Lane and ride for 1¼ miles to the T-junction. **Turn R**, down the hill, and return to the car park in Bramley.

*Boats on the Wey at Millmead*

## BRAMLEY

Bramley was a Saxon settlement and was recorded in Domesday as having the largest and most valuable manor in Surrey. William the Conqueror handed it to Bishop Odo and there is a carved village plaque outside the library to commemorate this. Bramley expanded in 1865 when the railway line from Guildford to Horsham opened, offering a station in Bramley. Sadly this was closed in the Beeching cuts 100 years later but the disused railway path provides an excellent wildlife corridor for walkers and cyclists. According to the *Guinness Book of Records*, the first women's cricket match was at the Bramley ground, Gosden Common, in 1745. This match was between the ladies of Bramley and those of the local village of Hascombe.

## GUILDFORD CATHEDRAL

It was proposed that Guildford Cathedral should be built when the diocese of Winchester became too large and was split into three. Some 183 architects submitted proposals and finally Edward Maufe's plans were selected in 1933 with a site on Stag Hill, high above Guildford. It was the very first cathedral to be built in the south since the Reformation but building had to cease during the Second World War and it was not until 1961 that it was consecrated, just one year before the consecration of the new Coventry Cathedral.

7

# Blackheath, Guildford and St Martha's

## *17 miles*

Ride from heathland along leafy lanes to the picturesque village of Shamley Green, with its large cricket green and duckpond. You can explore the attractive Cook Shop or relax on a seat at the Red Lion before cycling on the Downs Link towards Guildford. Here you cycle beside the River Wey as it flows towards Stoke Lock and on to Riverside Park Nature Reserve with its wetland and man-made lake. At Pewley Down there are stunning views southwards to the Chantries and Chilworth. Should you decide to detour and walk to the top of St Martha's Hill, yet more extensive vistas await.

**Maps:** OS Landranger 186 Aldershot and Guildford, OS Explorer 145 Guildford and Farnham (GR TQ036461).

**Starting point:** Blackheath car park. From Guildford take the A281 Horsham road, turn left at Shalford and follow the A248 towards Dorking. Turn right over the level crossing opposite the Percy Arms in Chilworth. Turn left in Blackheath to the car park at the far end of the road.

**By train:** Chilworth station is on the route and Guildford station is close by.

**Refreshments:** In Shamley Green there are two pubs, the Red Lion and the Bricklayers, and the Jeni Wren Cook Shop serves coffee overlooking the green. At Shalford there is the atmospheric gastro pub, the Seahorse. Guildford offers numerous options including the White House and the YMCA restaurant by the towpath. The Percy Arms is at Chilworth and the Villagers is at Blackheath.

**The route:** About two-thirds of the ride is off-road on river towpaths, the Downs Link, and paths and tracks where it is often quite flat. There are some undulations around Blackheath and a long gradual climb up to Pewley Down from Stoke Park. Parts of the river towpath may have muddy patches after rain and there are a few steps to negotiate on a bridge over the River Wey.

Ride down to the village crossroads and **turn L** up the hill. In just over a mile **turn R** at a T-junction into Northcote Lane and in under ¾ mile cross the B2128 to ride into the lane to pass Lord's Hill. Shortly **turn R** into NCN22, or detour to explore the village of Shamley Green by **turning L**. Back on NCN22, ride ½ mile to go over the canal to the bridge.

**Turn right** sharply to climb up to the Downs Link, the disused railway track, in the direction of Bramley and Guildford. At Bramley you can visit the Jolly Farmer, to your left in the village.

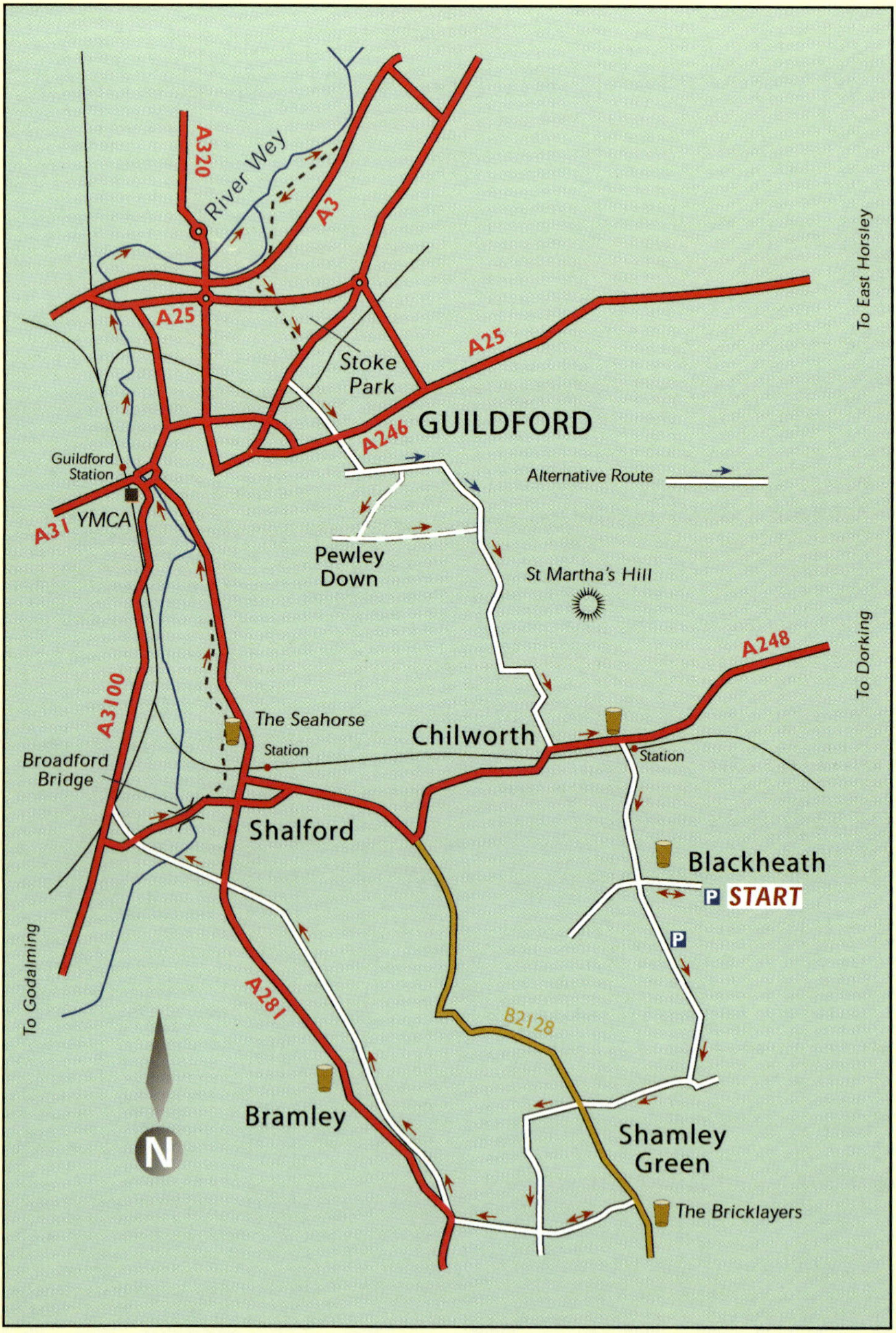

# 7 Blackheath, Guildford and St Martha's

A320
River Wey
A3
A25
A25
Stoke Park
GUILDFORD
A246
Guildford Station
YMCA
A31
Alternative Route
Pewley Down
St Martha's Hill
To East Horsley
To Dorking
A248
A3100
The Seahorse
Station
Chilworth
Station
Broadford Bridge
Shalford
Blackheath
START
A281
B2128
To Godalming
Bramley
Shamley Green
The Bricklayers
N

St Martha's Hill from Lockner Farm

Otherwise go ahead for 1½ miles, crossing the A281 and the River Wey. Near Peasmarsh go beneath the road bridge and immediately **bear R** to follow the shared path beside the A248 to cross the Wey at Broadford Bridge, Shalford, the NCN22.

Soon **turn L** into a track and then **half R** into a path across Shalford Common past cottages. Keep ahead over the railway bridge and ride almost 1¼ miles towards Guildford on the shared path, past the rear entrance to the attractive Seahorse pub and right through Shalford Park to the bridge over the River Wey. Cross here and ride along beside the river to the Guildford lock. **Bear L** to cross the small bridge into Bury Fields.

Follow the river for about 2¼ miles as it flows on to Riverside Park. On the way you can enjoy refreshment with a river view at the YMCA restaurant up an outside stairway on your left, and soon the National Trust's Dapdune Wharf is on the opposite bank. Go up to the Guildford bypass and cross to ride on the right-hand bank. Next cross the A320, the Woking road, to follow the river. Riverside Park starts just past Stoke Lock, the oldest lock in Surrey.

After about ⅓ mile from Stoke Lock **turn R** across a boardwalk where pushing your bike is recommended. The water and vegetation look positively Amazonian. **Turn R** onto a path, go through gates, and return towards Guildford past the large man-made lake and the nature reserve. After more gates follow the main path as it bends sharply left and upwards, then **turn R** into a path under the A3 to emerge at the rear of Spectrum, the Guildford Sports Centre. **Bear R**

*A colourful narrowboat on the Wey*

to cross the bypass and go into Stoke Park.

Soon **bear half L** across the park and cross the London Road. **Turn R** and after 200 yards **turn L** into Cross Lanes and go over the railway bridge. A path, still Cross Lanes, lies straight ahead between houses. Cross two roads and you reach Warren Road. Alternatively, use roughly parallel surfaced roads, Maori Road and Albury Road. **Turn L** into Warren Road.

**Either:** take the pretty way and see the stunning views from Pewley Down over the Chantries. Shortly, opposite Rose Trees, turn downwards into a lane towards Warren Farm. Soon **turn R** into a footpath and push your bike up to Pewley Down. Turn to look over your shoulder at the views over north Guildford and the cathedral on the way. **Turn L** along the ridge and go onto a path leading to Longdown. **Turn R** into Halfpenny Lane.
**Or:** easier, but without the views, continue on Warren Road/One Tree Hill for a mile, keeping ahead into Halfpenny Lane when the road bends sharply left.

Go down the hill and up a small rise towards St Martha's car park. Consider parking your bike and walking to the top of the hill. The church, which is on the Pilgrims' Way from Winchester to Canterbury, may not be open but the views to the south are stupendous. For the route, continue down the narrow lane passing Chilworth Manor and winding into Blacksmith Lane. **Turn L** at the T-junction onto the A248 to the Percy Arms. **Turn R**

*Summer flowers on Pewley Down*

across the level crossing and climb up Sample Oak Lane to Blackheath. **Turn L** at the crossroads and the car park is at the end of the road.

## DAPDUNE WHARF, GUILDFORD

This is National Trust-owned and has a Visitor Centre which can be accessed by crossing the footbridge in front of the railway bridge and backtracking on the eastern river bank. You can see where the huge Wey barges were built and climb aboard *Reliance*, which was built in 1931 and could carry up to 80 tons of cargo. She traded between Guildford and the London Docks prior to her collision with Cannon Street Bridge in 1968.

## RIVERSIDE PARK

Extending from near Stoke Lock to Burpham, this is a narrow nature corridor. Surprisingly the reserve exists as a result of the building of the six-lane A3 in the late 1970s when agricultural land was purchased by Guildford Borough Council for the construction of the road. The lake was a by-product of the gravel extraction. Wetland is comparatively rare and so the park provides an important habitat for a diverse range of birds, amphibians and insects, with meadow and woodland for various flora and fauna such as skylarks. The open water is used by breeding and wintering birds such as snipe and kingfisher, as well as offering a sizeable lake for freshwater fish. Birds are a particular feature of the site which is managed in conjunction with the British Trust for Ornithology.

# 8

# Newlands Corner, Blackheath and Shere

*15 miles*

Newlands Corner is a well-known beauty spot on the North Downs with panoramic views to the south. To the west is the small church of St Martha which lies upon a hilltop on the Pilgrims' Way. Its position is central to the ride and the characteristic outline of the church, with pines alongside, can be seen from various vantage points. From the North Downs ridge you drop down to Shalford Park and return via the attractive villages of Blackheath, with its gloriously situated cricket ground, Albury, noted for its tall, ornamental chimneys, and the picturesque, oft filmed, Shere.

**Maps:** OS Landranger 186 Aldershot and Guildford and 187 Dorking and Reigate, OS Explorer 145 Guildford and Farnham (GR TQ042492).

**Starting point:** The car park at Newlands Corner. From Guildford follow signs towards Dorking and the A25. Turn right at the traffic lights at West Clandon and Newlands Corner car park is at the top of the hill on the right-hand side.

**By train:** Chilworth or Shalford stations are on the route. Guildford station is just over a mile away.

**Refreshments:** There is the Barn Café, or the kiosk in the car park, for snacks at Newlands Corner. The Seahorse is at Shalford, whilst in all of the villages there are pubs, such as the White Horse and the Willian Bray at Shere and the Drummond Arms at Albury. The Lucky Duck café in Shere offers light meals and teas.

**The route:** There is a long gentle downward slope of 4¾ miles from the North Downs ridge above Shere towards Shalford Park. The return is a mixture of flat riding, an undulating section around Blackheath and there are two steep climbs from Albury and from Shere back up to the North Downs. About half is off-road, with some riding on the 30 mph speed restricted A248. The A25 is crossed twice.

From Newlands Corner car park, with the views to your left, cycle for about a mile along the main trackway. When the track peters out, **bear L** onto one of the narrow exit paths to White Lane, where you **turn R**. Keep straight ahead and cross into Longdown Road where the road swings sharply to the right. Go into the path and through to Pewley Down. Here you can admire

*The delightful village of Shere*

both the variety of chalk downland flowers and a superb vista of the Surrey Hills. Take a short deviation to your right, to see far-reaching views over the north of Guildford to the cathedral.

**Bear L** near the end of the Downs and take one of the paths that leads sharply downwards, probably pushing your bike. Cycle down Northdown Lane and, still heading downwards, go onto the Pilgrims' Way to the A281, the Guildford to Horsham road. Cross at the bollard into Shalford Park. **Turn L** and, using the cycle path, continue to Shalford. You pass the Thames Water Treatment works and, shortly afterwards, watch out for the concealed rear entrance to the Seahorse. If you feel like a break, the Seahorse is an attractive and popular gastro pub.

Go over the railway bridge, **turn L** on the track to Shalford. Cross over into King's Road then immediately **turn R** into Chinthurst Lane. Cycle for 1¾ miles and **turn L** into the T-junction towards Wonersh. The village has some beautiful half-timbered and tile-hung houses, as well as the 16th-century inn, the Grantley Arms. **Turn R** to pass the pub and then immediately **turn L** into Barnett Lane. **Turn R** at the T-junction at the end of the lane and climb towards Blackheath.

In a mile, St Martin's church, to your right, is modelled on an Italian wayside chapel and has beautiful waterglass murals to admire. **Turn L** at the crossroads in Blackheath village unless you wish to visit the Villagers pub ahead, or the cricket ground on the heath set in idyllic surroundings. Ride to Chilworth passing the Franciscan friary on your left. Cross the level crossing and **turn R** on the A248 towards Albury.

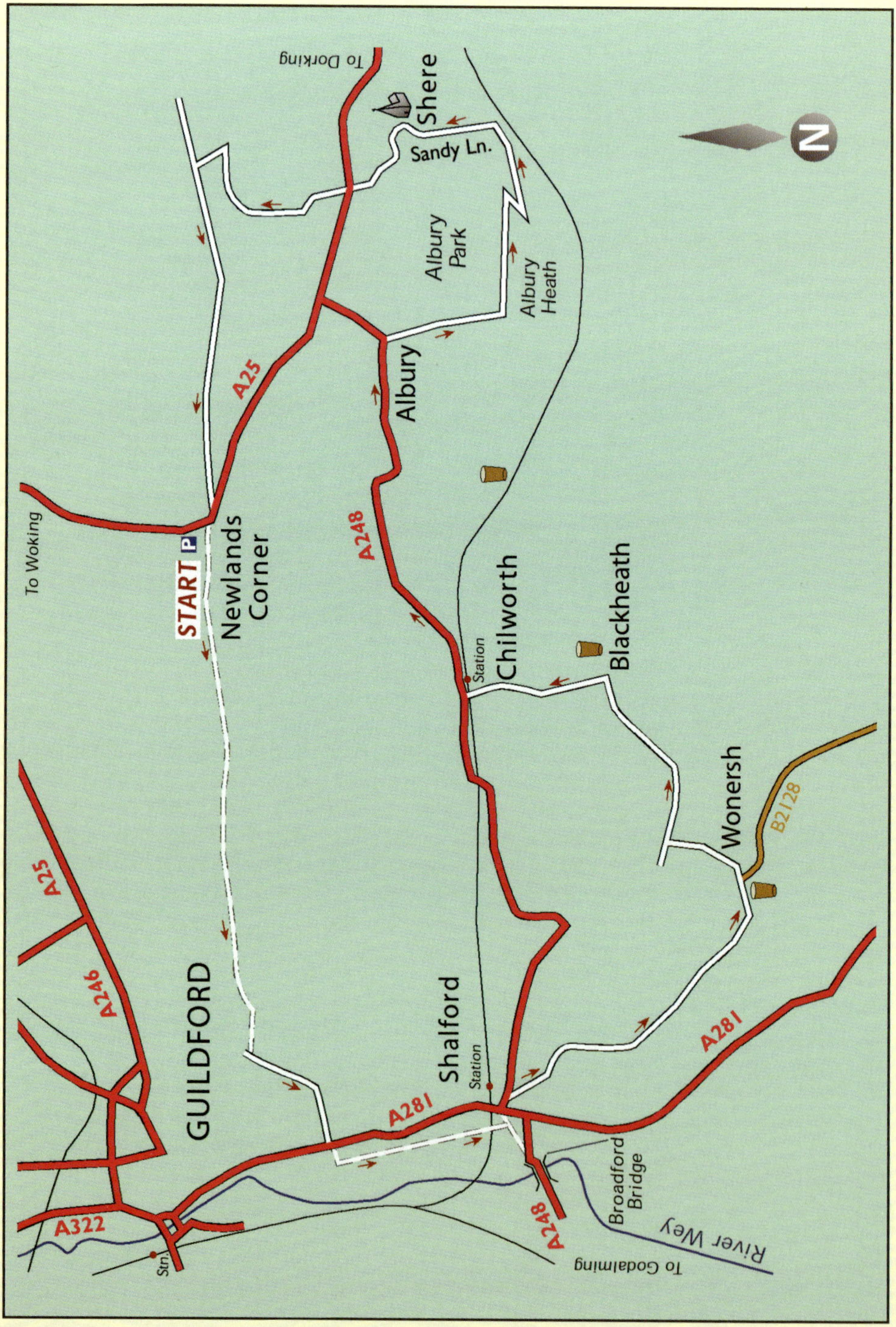

# 8 Newlands Corner, Blackheath and Shere

To Dorking
Shere
Sandy Ln.
Albury Park
Albury Heath
Albury
A25
A248
To Woking
START
P
Newlands Corner
Chilworth
Station
Blackheath
Wonersh
B2128
A25
A246
GUILDFORD
Shalford
Station
A281
A281
Broadford Bridge
A248
A322
Stn.
River Wey
To Godalming

The ride now follows the Tillingbourne valley, which runs to the southern side of the Downs. The Tillingbourne stream is evident in Albury, as you cross the bridge, and can be enjoyed in the garden of the Drummond Arms. The stream runs into the fishing lakes further on to your left. **Turn R** as the main road turns sharply to the left and climb New Road. At the top of the hill, **turn L** along Park Road to pass Albury Heath. In a little over a mile **turn L** at the T-junction and descend to the village of Shere. Try one of the pubs or the Lucky Duck café where you sit outside in the garden on a sunny day. St James's church is well worth a visit and you can find out more about the anchoress of Shere (see below).

**Turn L** at the T-junction and pedal out of the village to the A25. Cross over at the off-set crossroads and climb for under a mile up Combe Lane. **Fork L** into Staple Lane and soon **turn L** into Drove Lane, the downward sloping trackway across the Downs. Follow this as you ride through woods to Newlands Corner. Cross the road back to the car park.

## NEWLANDS CORNER

Although just 567 ft high, on a clear day it is claimed that you can see five counties. Walk down the hill for a couple of hundred yards where the views open out over cornfields, towards the Greensand Ridge and St Martha's church. There are many ancient yews and a document signed by the Archbishop of Canterbury in 1988 attests to a particular tree being 2,000 years old.

## SHERE AND THE ANCHORESS

One of the most visited and filmed villages in Surrey, Shere is a gem. The clear Tillingbourne stream runs past back gardens and past Lower Street, where the Shere ducks are a particular feature. It is a village of picturesque half-timbered 18th-century and Victorian houses whilst the White Horse Inn dates back further to the 16th century. The beautiful 12th-century church of St James stands upon an even earlier 7th-century site. In 1329 Christine Carpenter, daughter of the Shere carpenter, decided to devote her life to God by living as an anchoress. She was bricked up in a tiny cell in the north wall of the church where she could see the altar through a narrow aperture. Later, it is said, she left her cell but in 1332, at Christine's request, the bishop allowed her to re-enter on the condition she would never be allowed to leave again. There is a book by Paul Moorcraft, and now a film, both of which are entitled *The Anchoress of Shere.*

## BLACKHEATH

The village lies on the edge of a heathland of heather and gorse, a Site of Special Scientific Interest, where efforts are made to maintain the heathland habitat in order to encourage ground-nesting birds, butterflies, beetles, adders and lizards. The village was a mere hamlet until 1867 when Sir William Chandler Roberts-Austen, Assayer of the Royal Mint, employed a fashionable architect, Charles Harrison Townsend, to build his house here, whereupon others soon followed. In the late 19th century Sir William commissioned the same architect to construct the village church by building on to a cottage that he had bought.

9

# Peaslake, Coldharbour and Westcott

*20 miles*

Ride into the picturesque village of Shere, climb to Coldharbour, one of the highest villages in the county, and sample cafés and traditional pubs along the way. The route runs through the heart of the Surrey Hills along winding leafy lanes, over hills with heady descents, and boasts far-reaching views to the South Downs. Visit the National Trust Rhododendron Wood, ablaze with colour in spring, admire the carpets of bluebells on Leith Hill's slopes and see Jack, the blacksmith, strike the hour on the famous Abinger clock.

**Maps:** OS Landranger 187 Dorking and Reigate, OS Explorers 146 Dorking, Box Hill and Reigate, 145 Guildford and Farnham (GR TQ088478).

**Starting point:** Gomshall station, 5 miles west of Dorking on the A25.

**By train:** Gomshall station.

**Refreshments:** In Shere there is the White Horse, the William Bray and the Lucky Duck café. In Peaslake try the Hurtwood Inn or the village stores for drinks and snacks. In Ewhurst, Forest Green, Coldharbour and Westcott there are pubs and at Abinger there is a tea room.

**The route:** There are quiet lanes and some bridleway riding to avoid the A25. This is in the midst of the Surrey hills so expect an ascent such as Forest Green to Leith Hill, where you climb the pretty but steep lane for ½ mile. Equally there are some good downhill runs, e.g. from Pitch Hill into Ewhurst and from Coldharbour to Wotton.

**Turn L** out of the station approach and **turn R** into Wonham Way, a footpath only, immediately after the bridge. Soon **turn R** into a bridleway at the bend and follow NCN22 signs all the way to Shere. Go under the bridge, **bear L** and in ¼ mile go straight ahead to cross Queen's Street into a driveway. **Fork R** into a bridleway and in ½ mile Shere church spire comes into view.

At the end of the track **turn R** to explore the picturesque village of Shere. Go past the church to the square and see the clear Tillingbourne stream with its ducks and then enjoy a coffee at the Lucky Duck or visit one of the pubs. Take the road upwards past the William Bray.

Climb the hill and at the top go over the railway bridge, leaving the NCN22. **Turn L** towards Peaslake. In a mile **turn R** into idyllic Jesses Lane. In a further mile **turn L** and soon **bear R** towards Peaslake village. This is a

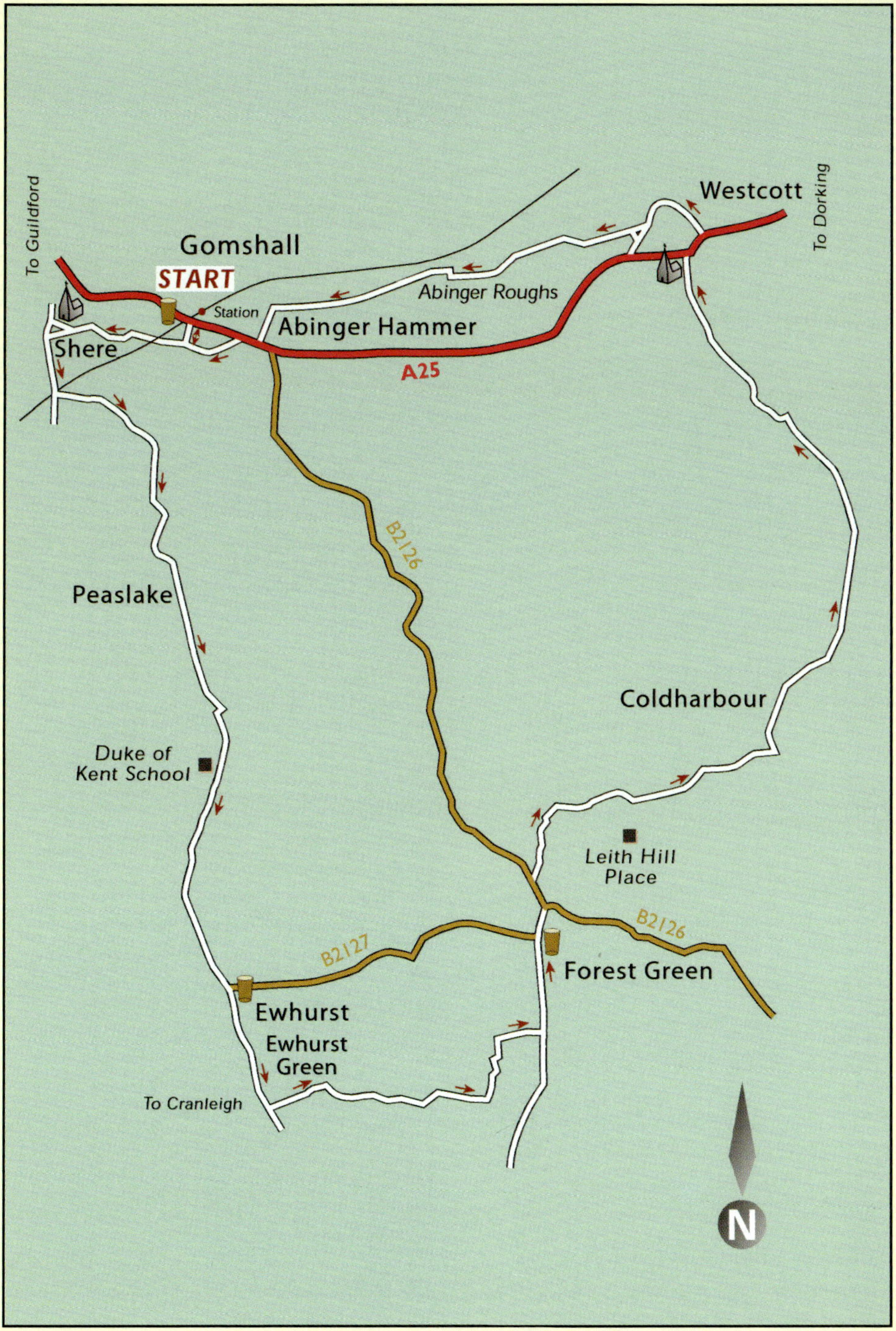

To Guildford
Gomshall
START
Station
Shere
Abinger Roughs
Abinger Hammer
A25
Westcott
To Dorking
B2126
Peaslake
Coldharbour
Duke of
Kent School
Leith Hill
Place
B2126
B2127
Forest Green
Ewhurst
Ewhurst
Green
To Cranleigh
N

*Cycling through Coldharbour village*

veritable biking mecca with a bike shop and the aroma of cheese straws drifting from the village stores. Alternatively you can sit at a table outside the Hurtwood Inn whilst you watch the world go by.

Take the major road, SP Ewhurst via Coverwood. In ¾ mile the road bends sharply to the right and climbs to pass the Duke of Kent school. Enjoy some glorious views as you ride along the ridge. Descend to the T-junction and **turn L** to sail down the hill towards Ewhurst. Perhaps pause at the Bull's Head and rest in the garden with its bright flower borders. Ride through the village on the B2127 and, at the corner, **turn L** (ahead) towards Ewhurst Green.

In ⅓ mile **turn L** into Plough Lane. Go over the hump-backed bridge and **turn R** by the post box into Lower Breache Road. In ¾ mile, at the end of a left-hand bend, **turn R** onto a bridleway through woods, ignoring a byway and a farm lane. **Turn L** by a cottage into Pond Head Lane. Soon pass a pond where you should see resident swans. Cycle ¾ mile on the bridleway. The last gate is electric and operated by a button on a post, well before the gate. **Turn L** and go to the attractive Parrot Inn. You can sit at a table outside and relax overlooking the cricket green.

**Turn R** at the major road, the B2127, and soon **L** onto the B2126, SP Holmbury St Mary. In ⅕ mile, at the top of the rise, **turn R** into Tanhurst Lane to climb the lane to the Rhododendron Wood, on the slopes of Leith Hill.

Cycle on to the junctions and go ahead towards Coldharbour for 2 miles. There

you can pause to gaze at the views or perhaps rest at the Plough. Continue for a further 2 miles as you enjoy the downhill run towards Dorking, but watch for Logmore Lane where you **fork L** at the end of the woods. Close to Westcott, **fork R** past the church and **turn R** into the A25. Soon **turn L** into Westcott Street, unless you are visiting the Crown Inn, ⅓ mile to your right, a good stop for those who enjoy home-made food.

The lane bends towards the A25 but **turn R** into a bridleway. Pedal past farmland for 1½ miles. The track narrows to a path and, looking back, the spire of Ranmore church can be seen to the north-east. Cross Abinger Lane and continue on the track through woods, the NCN22, and over Abinger Roughs. In ¾ mile there is a large grass area with a seat which makes an excellent picnic spot. Keep straight on into a narrow path.

**Turn L** into Hackhurst Lane to cycle down to the A25. To your left is the Abinger tea rooms where you can have a light meal or sample Annie's delicious cakes. Notice the famous Abinger clock on the corner.

**Turn R** from Hackhurst Lane onto the A25. In a short distance **turn L** into the

*The Leith Hill road*

*The attractive village of Peaslake*

bridleway to pass Southbrook Farm to Wonham Way. **Turn R** and go down to the A25 by Gomshall station.

## SHERE

See route 8.

## PEASLAKE

Peaslake nestles in the Hurtwood on the northern slopes of the greensand ridge. The village has both a popular village shop and bicycle shop, as well as a doctor's surgery, church and the Hurtwood Inn. Walkers and mountain bikers are drawn to this unique spot as the surrounding access land offers superb countryside and glorious views from the top of Holmbury Hill. St Mark's church, which replaced an inadequate Mission Room, was consecrated in 1889. The site was donated by the Lord of the Manor, whilst George Cubitt contributed £1,000. The Misses Spottiswoode, from Shere, gave the organ and churchyard fence. The church is built of local sandstone and much of the carving was carried out by local craftsmen.

## LEITH HILL AND COLDHARBOUR

Leith Hill, at 967 ft, is the highest hill in Surrey and the tower at the top raises it to 1,000 ft, technically making it a mountain. The road that winds around the upper slopes to the tiny village of Coldharbour is a gem. It snakes around beautiful woodland with carpets of bluebells in spring and affords glimpses to the South Downs. Leith Hill Place was the childhood home of Ralph Vaughan Williams, the celebrated composer and conductor of the Leith Hill festival. The house had been bought by his great-great-grandfather, Josiah Wedgwood, of Wedgwood Pottery, in the mid 19th century and Charles Darwin, Vaughan William's great-uncle, would visit the house for holidays.

10

# Shere, Farley Green and Pitch Hill

## *12 or 17 miles*

A ride in the heart of the Surrey Hills, in glorious countryside. The route runs through the woodland of Peaslake and Winterfold and passes the sandy heathland of Shere and Farley Green. Explore the 12th-century church in Shere, wander by the half-timbered houses and see the ducks on the rushing Tillingbourne stream. Visit Peaslake, an attractive village and a mecca for cyclists, followed by a rare 3-mile descent through woodland from Winterfold into Farley Green. If taking the longer route, you return via the Downs Link to linger in the picturesque village of Shamley Green with its large cricket green, pubs and a cook shop.

**Maps:** OS Landrangers 186 Aldershot and Guildford and 187 Dorking and Reigate, OS Explorers 145 Guildford and Farnham, 146 Dorking, Box Hill and Reigate (GR TQ073479).

**Starting point:** Shere village car park. From the A25 from Guildford turn right into Shere village. The car park is on your left just before Middle Street.

**By train:** Gomshall station is 1 mile from the start.

**Refreshments:** The Lucky Duck, the White Horse and the William Bray in Shere, the Hurtwood Inn in Peaslake and the village shop serves hot drinks and snacks. The William IV is at Little London. At Shamley Green are the Bricklayers and the Red Lion, as well as the Cook Shop which serves coffee at an outside table.

**The route:** The main route is on quiet roads, lanes and about 1 mile off-road near Shere. This is the heart of the Surrey Hills so there are climbs, but only the short sharp ⅕ mile to Winterfold is extreme. The long descent makes it all worthwhile! The longer route has 1¾ miles of off-road riding along the Downs Link and a bridleway followed by a climb to Farley Green.

From Shere village car park, cross the road and ride past the shops in Middle Street unless you are craving an early coffee or a breakfast, when you may wish to stop at the Lucky Duck on your right. **Turn L** and, after St James' church, **bear R** and up Church Lane. Soon **turn L** into the track at the top, and with the church spire to your left, ride ahead along the grassy path which is the NCN22. In ½ mile **bear L** along a driveway towards the road.

**Turn R** into Burrows Lane and go over the level crossing and up the hill. At the top, cross obliquely into Lawbrook Lane and ride for ¾ mile. This is a beautiful ride through rolling fields.

## Shere, Farley Green and Pitch Hill

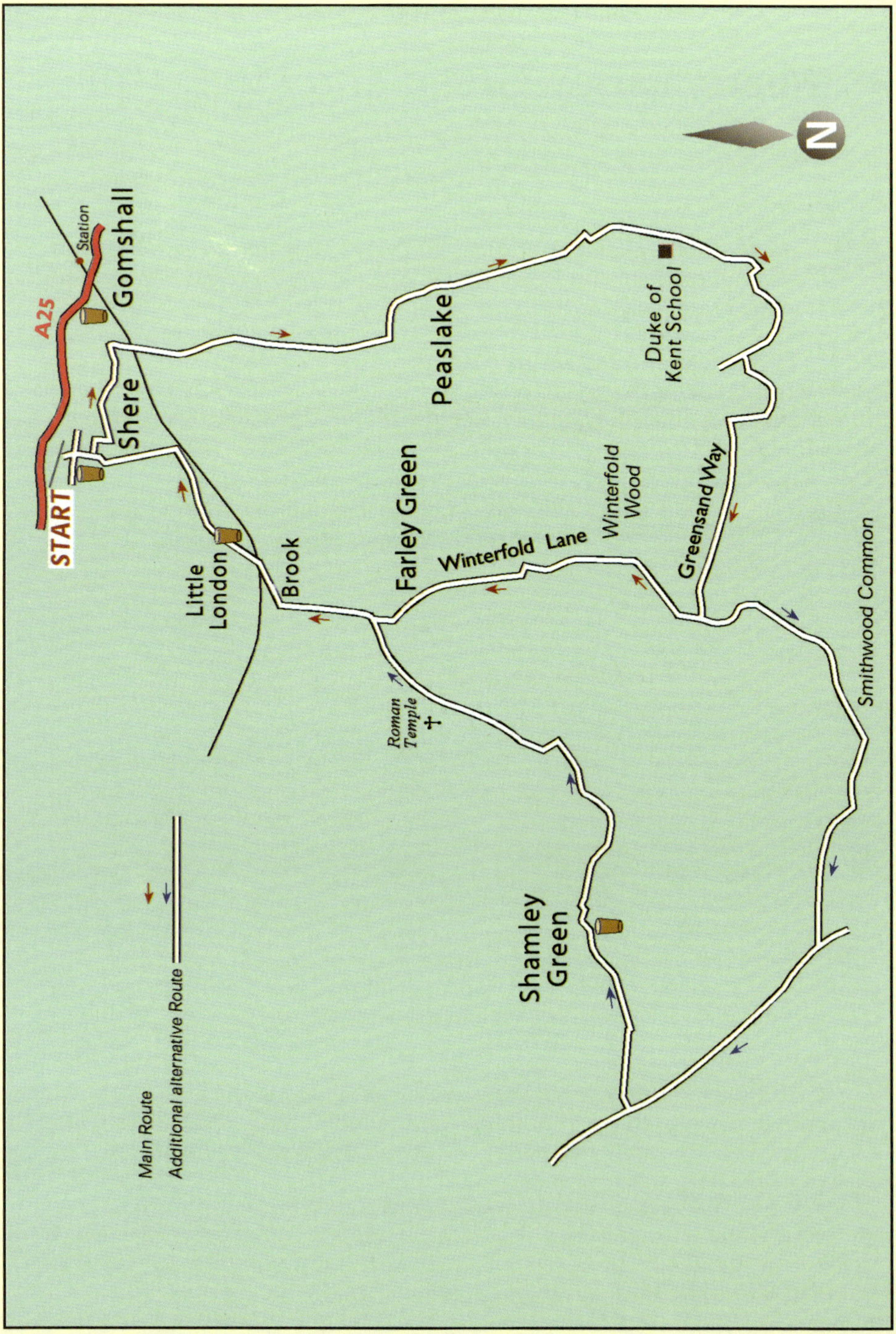

N

Gomshall
Station
A25
Shere
START
Little London
Brook
Farley Green
Peaslake
Duke of Kent School
Winterfold Wood
Winterfold Lane
Greensand Way
Smithwood Common
Roman Temple
Shamley Green

Main Route
Additional alternative Route

*Cheery flowerpot residents in Shere*

**Turn L** and in ¼ mile **bear R** towards Peaslake. Not only is there a cycle shop but the village shop sells freshly-baked cheese straws, as well as other goodies such as snacks and drinks. For a longer break sample the comfortable atmosphere of the Hurtwood Inn.

Leave the village southwards, SP Ewhurst, via Coverwood. In ¾ mile the road bends sharply to the right and climbs to pass the Duke of Kent School. Ride for ½ mile further enjoying some glorious views from the ridge.

At the brow **turn R** up a narrow lane towards the major road. **Turn R** and pass the Windmill pub. **Turn immediately L** into the Warren, a residential lane. **Or:** make a diversion to the car park on your right where you could lock your bike and climb to the top of Pitch Hill. The views across the Weald to the South Downs are stunning.

The lane is partially unsurfaced, but continue to a junction and **turn R** for ⅕ mile up the steepest hill in this book! **Turn L** at the top, past Reynards Hill, and follow the narrow lane past Winterfold to wind downwards for over a mile to a junction.

**Either: turn R** for the main route. Enjoy the long run down to Farley Green, at first past pine forests, where it is said that some of the hidden loot from the Great Train Robbery was found. This is a gentle 2-mile run down into Farley Green where you should **turn R**.

**Or: turn L** for the longer route, from Winterfold down to Smithwood Common. **Turn R** along Rushett Common and **R** on the major road. **Turn L** at the roundabout and in just over ½ mile find a narrow path on your left, running parallel to the road. In ¼ mile **turn R** onto the Downs Link.

*On the way to Farley Heath*

In 1⅓ miles, before a bridge, descend to **turn R** across the Wey and Arun Canal on the NCN22 to Shamley Green. Take the road ahead, the SCW, up to Farley Heath where there is a car park on the left. Soon there are the ruins of a Roman temple where the ground plan has been laid out in stone. Ride down to Farley Green and rejoin the main route.

Ride for ½ mile towards Brook. At the lowest point **turn R** towards Little London. This rural lane is a gem which winds its way from Brook past fields and attractive houses. Pedal beneath the railway and then past the attractive William IV pub. **Bear R** at the junction to cycle nearly ½ mile past Shere Heath to the railway bridge. **Turn L** here into Sandy Lane towards Shere and return to the car park.

## FARLEY GREEN

Farley Green, a rural village in the Surrey Hills, has a claim to fame in that the foundations of a Roman temple are marked out on nearby Farley Heath. In 1839 Martin Tupper exposed some evidence of remains on the site and, after many subsequent attempts, in 1995 archaeologists were able to provide a ground plan of the temple. There is an artist's impression of how the site might have looked 2,000 years ago.

The tiny church of St Michael is tucked away down a track leading off Shophouse Lane, your road to the green. It is an 18th-century traditional, black weather-boarded barn which was given as a chapel of ease in 1929 by the widowed Clara Courtenay-Wells, in memory of her late husband. One day during the Second World War, when church bells were only to be rung in the event of invasion, the single bell of St Michael's was heard tolling continuously. It turned out that a wandering cow had got her horn entangled in the bell rope!

## SHAMLEY GREEN

At the centre of this picturesque village is the large green bisected by the road. On one side is the cricket green and village stores and on the other, a duck pond, the 18th-century Red Lion pub and an interesting cook shop in which to browse. Elegant Victorian houses are set around the green, as well as older tile-hung cottages. The second pub, the Bricklayers, is at the southern end of the village and the 19th-century Christ Church is on the brow of the hill. The village's claim to fame in the world of celebrity is that Sir Richard Branson was born and spent his childhood here and Tony Hart, the artist, lived here for many years.

**SHERE** is described in Route 8.

11

# Holmbury St Mary, Ellen's Green and Friday Street

## *23 miles, with 9 or 15 mile alternatives*

There are well-known beauty spots on this ride such as Friday Street, with its beautiful hammer pond on the lower slopes of Leith Hill, and Holmbury St Mary, which clings to the slopes of Holmbury Hill. A village green is always a welcome feature and you will see fine examples at Ewhurst Green, Ockley and Forest Green. It would be surprising if you did not see at least one game of cricket underway, should you pass by on a summer Sunday. The ride is peppered with good pubs, pretty hamlets and villages, waterscapes and shady lanes.

**Maps:** OS Landranger 187 Dorking and Reigate, OS Explorers 146 Dorking, Box Hill and Reigate, 134 Crawley and Horsham (GR TQ124415).

**Starting point:** The car park at the Parrot, Forest Green. From the A24 Dorking to Horsham road take the A29 at the Beare Green roundabout to Ockley. Turn right onto the B2126. At Forest Green fork left to the Parrot.

**By train:** Ockley station is less than a mile from the route.

**Refreshments:** The Stephan Langton is at Friday Street, the King's Head and the Royal Oak at Holmbury St Mary, the Wheatsheaf at Ellen's Green and the Punch Bowl at Okewood Hill. There are various pubs in Ockley to choose from, and don't forget the Parrot!

**The route:** This is a good hilly ride but after a climb to Leith Hill the hills are shorter and there are some long descents. Most of the route is on quiet roads and lanes. There are sections of off-road riding around Vann Lake and Ockley. Should conditions be very damp, ignore paragraphs 6 to 8 and go ahead on Weare Street. At the T-junction turn left onto the B2126, and remain upon it to Forest Green.

**To shorten the route:** Use the B2126 to make a northern hilly ride (9 miles) or a southern circuit for a more gentle ride (15 miles).

**Turn R** out of the car park and **R** again onto the B2126. In ¾ mile **turn L** to climb towards Leith Hill, passing Etherley Farm. Keep onwards at the road junction unless you wish to turn sharp left to explore the glorious National Trust Rhododendron Wood, in season in spring. In ¼ mile at Starveal car park you could detour **R** along the Greensand Way, and either cycle or

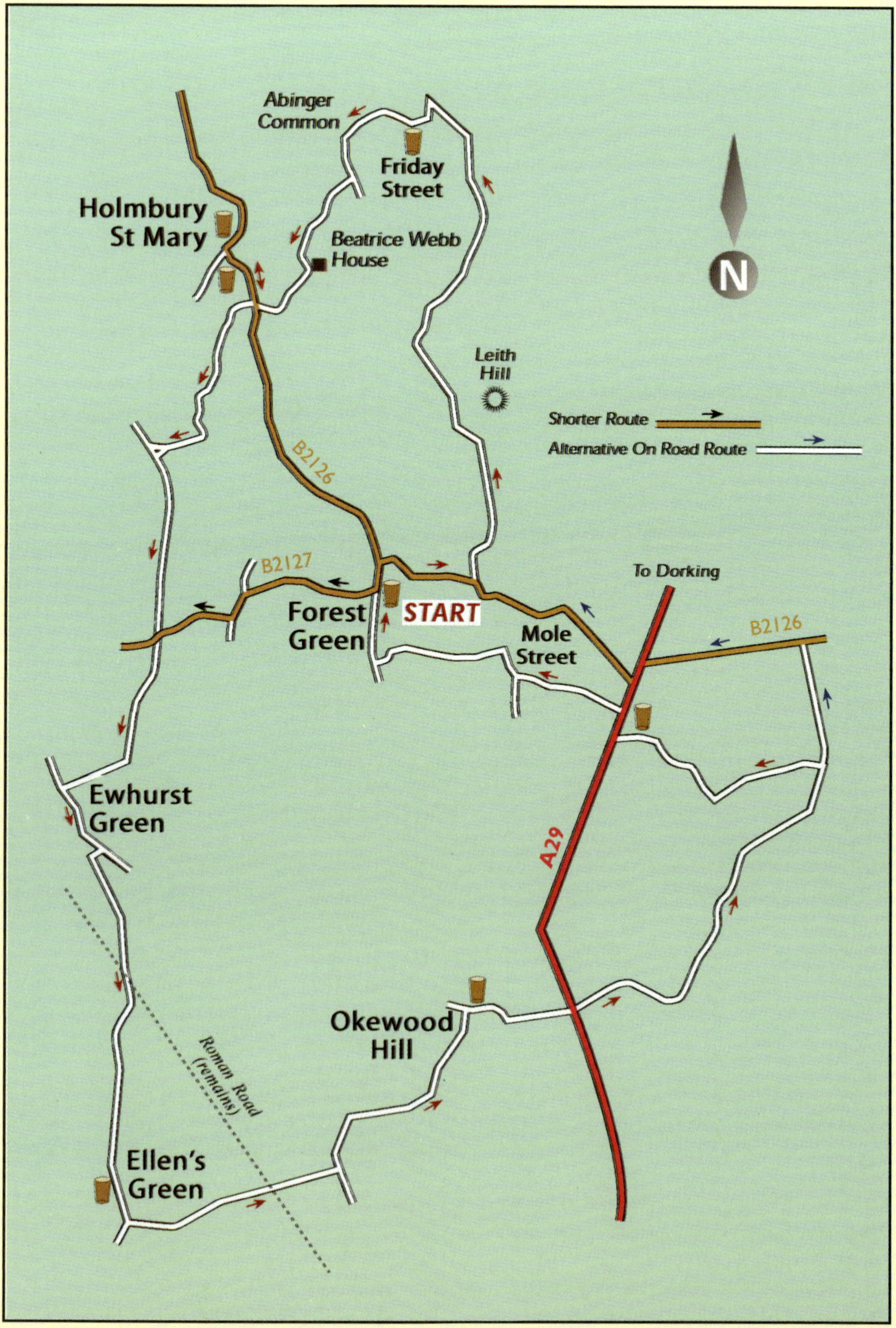

# 11 Holmbury St Mary, Ellen's Green and Friday Street

*Along the way near Gosterwood Manor Farm*

walk to the top of Leith Hill and the Tower. The views are outstanding and you are upon the highest hill in Surrey.

In ½ mile from the car park, **fork R**, SP Friday Street. This is a lovely ride through wooded countryside and provides a gentle descent. In 1½ miles **turn L**, SP Friday Street. At the base of the hill is the beautiful Friday Street pond. To visit the Stephan Langton pub, turn left along the lane. From the pond, climb the short, sharp hill and soon reach a major road near Abinger Common. **Turn L** and then *second* **R**, SP Holmbury St Mary. The Beatrice Webb House lies up a driveway to your left opposite Belmont School. Descend the narrow winding hill to Holmbury St Mary.

Your route lies ahead into Pitland Street at a staggered junction. To detour to the village **turn R** and the green is ½ mile away in front of the church of St Mary and the Royal Oak pub. Back on the route, the King's Head pub is shortly to your right. Continue up the hill and follow the meandering Holmbury Hill Road. There is a glorious view on the left after you have climbed past the Mullard Space Laboratory. **Turn L** at the T-junction by Hurtwood House School and go down the hill, past the model Lukyns Farm, with its prize-winning Poll Dorset sheep.

**Turn R** into the B2127 and immediately **L** into Plough Lane, a delightful rural gem. Continue for 1¼ miles over the small bridge to Ewhurst Green. **Turn L** at the T-junction and in ½ mile **turn R** into Summersbury Lane and ride for 1½ miles. At the B2128 **turn L** and soon the Wheatsheaf pub is on your right at Ellen's Green.

*The tranquil hammer pond at Friday Street*

Soon **turn L** along Furzen Lane to follow the SCW for the next 6 miles. In detail: climb the gradual incline of Furzen Lane and at the major road **turn L**. In ⅓ mile **turn R** and continue to the Punch Bowl Inn at Okewood Hill. This is another historic and attractive pub, complete with inglenook and stone floor, dating back to the 16th century. Descend for a few yards and **turn R**. Go down the hill towards the A29, passing the Surrey Union Hunt kennels. Cross the main road and go into Weare Street. This is a shady, quiet, meandering lane which you follow for 2½ miles.

(See the note in the box above if conditions are wet.) At the sign to Vann Lake, **turn L** along the drive, leaving the SCW. In 1 mile there is Vann Lake reserve, an Area of Special Scientific Interest. The track descends steeply for a few yards towards a bridge over the lake where you may see a cascading waterfall. Keep ahead on the narrowing path until you reach the house, Vann Croft, on your left. Continue on the driveway to the A29 and Ockley.

Cross over and **turn R** along the pathway towards the village and the old village pump. The Inn on the Green is on your right but **turn L** for the route, which goes to a bridge over a stream. Ride across the grass to the left of a large oak tree and pedal on to the trees. Look for the signpost and **bear L** along the bridleway which winds through the trees to Mole Street.

**Turn R** into Mole Street and in ½ mile **turn L** up the hill, and past Gosterwood Manor Farm. There is a fine view to the right of Leith Hill and the North Downs. Go down the hill and on through a gate. **Turn R** onto the road and the Parrot is soon on your right.

## HOLMBURY ST MARY

The village which is mainly Victorian, is built on the slopes of Holmbury Hill and the Hurtwood. Once called Felday, the village became known as Holmbury St Mary when George Edward Street, the Victorian architect of the Royal Courts of Justice in the Strand, designed and paid for the present parish church. He did this in memory of his second wife who died the same year they were married. It is a village well known for its first-class walking country, pubs and its youth hostel.

## FRIDAY STREET

This is a peaceful hamlet nestling in a valley in the woods, beside a large tranquil pond. Friday Street had an industrial past and was a centre for Wealden ironworking. The large man-made hammer pond suggests that in the 16th and 17th centuries it would have been used to drive the bellows for the smelting of iron and for powering the hammers for beating the metal. Stephan Langton, the 13th-century Archbishop of Canterbury, is said to have been born in the area and to have come to blows with King John near Friday Street. The pub, the Stephan Langton, is now named after the Archbishop.

12

# Reigate Heath, Brockham and Leigh

*15 or 10½ miles*

Skirting the periphery of the Surrey Hills area, this ride has the benefit of ever-changing views to the North Downs, pastoral countryside and attractive villages. The highlights include Reigate Heath windmill, where there is a chapel in the roundhouse, and the charming villages of Brockham, Betchworth, and Buckland with its wonderful deli. It is a route where you pedal by streams and green fields, you can detour to a village such as Leigh with its pub, explore delicious culinary distractions and maybe just stop to sit and admire the glorious backdrop of the North Downs ridge from the famous green at Brockham.

**Maps:** OS Landranger 187 Dorking and Reigate, OS Explorer 146 Dorking, Box Hill and Reigate (GR TQ239502).

**Starting point:** Flanchford Road, Reigate Heath. From the centre of Reigate take the A25 towards Dorking and turn first left by the pub, the Black Horse. There are soon car parks on both sides of the road.

**By train:** Reigate station is 1¼ miles from the route. Dorking and Deepdene stations are about a mile from the longer route.

**Refreshments:** There is plenty of opportunity for a choice of refreshments in all the villages en route. There is the Red Lion at Betchworth, the Duke's Head and the Royal Oak at Brockham, as well as the village deli and shop at Buckland, where you can have hot drinks in the garden. The Seven Stars is at Dawesgreen and the Skimmington Castle at Reigate Heath offers home-made food.

**The route:** There is a mixture of on- and off-road riding with a few undulations and one or two short climbs but it is a pleasant, gentle route. There are no main A-roads to cross and it is relatively quiet as far as traffic is concerned. A loop from Brockham, paragraph 3, can be omitted in order to shorten the route by 4½ miles.

Turn out of the car park, away from the A25. At the golf club you can detour to visit the windmill by turning right. The unusual roundhouse chapel is described below. Continuing on Flanchford Road, **turn first R** at the bottom of the hill into a track, a permissive horse ride. In about 150 yards **turn sharp L** passing Ivy Cottage and continue for ½ mile to a stream. **Fork L** and climb the pretty lane passing the Granary with its colourful summer flowers. At the top of the hill it would be a pity to miss the delightful

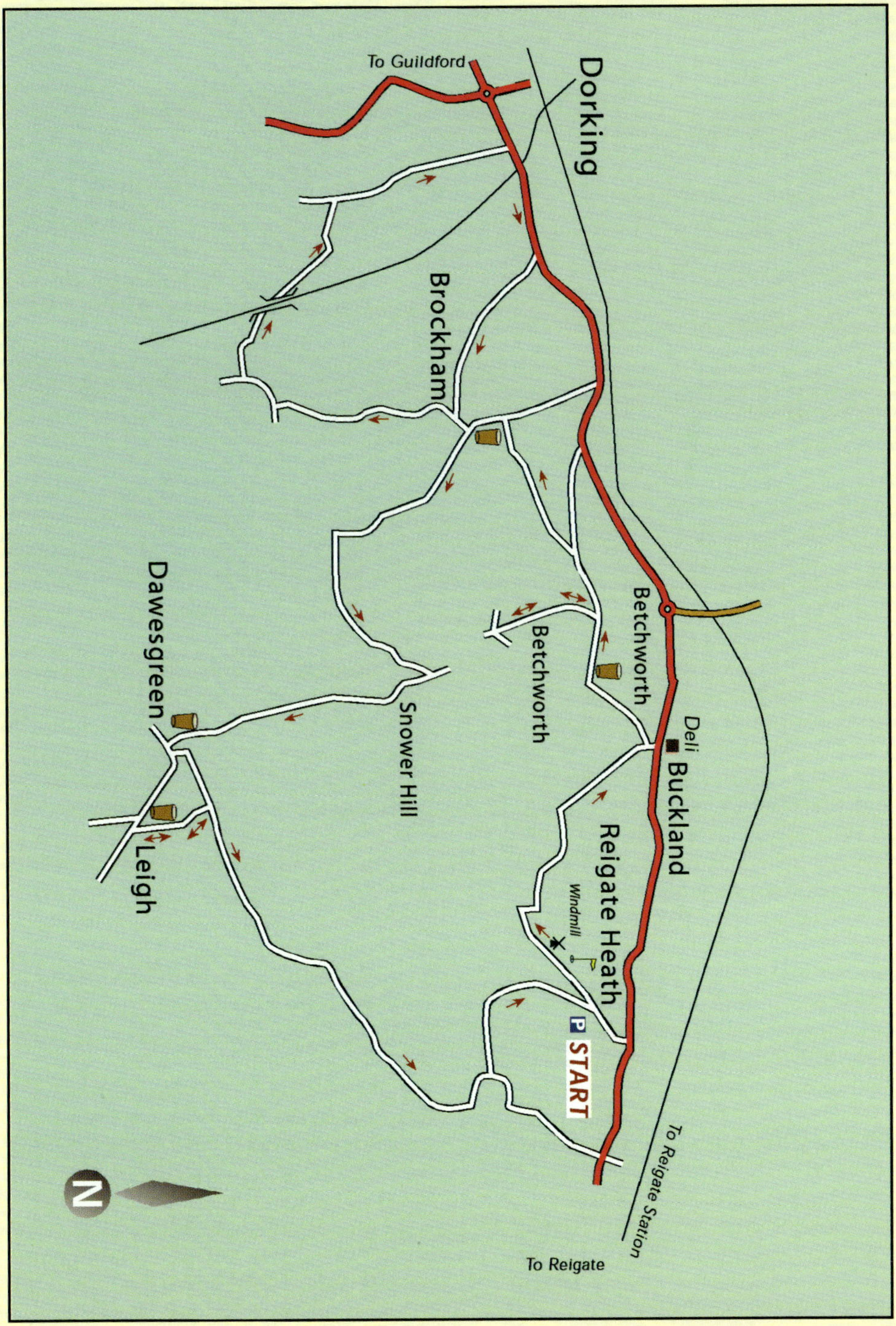

To Guildford
Dorking
Brockham
Dawesgreen
Leigh
Snower Hill
Betchworth
Betchworth
Deli
Buckland
Reigate Heath
Windmill
P
START
To Reigate Station
To Reigate
N

The village pond at Buckland

Buckland Deli where you can browse among the gifts and have drinks and delicious pastries in the tiny garden.

**Turn L** into Old Road and ride for 1 mile before **forking L** into Kiln Lane. On the way you pass the Red Lion and can make a short detour by turning left into picturesque Betchworth village, where there is St Michael's church which retains a fragment from Saxon times, the Dolphin pub and a forge. Cycle for ¾ mile down Kiln Lane past the sports fields before **turning L** to cross the River Mole into the attractive village of Brockham.

**Either:** Omit this paragraph and go straight to the green at Brockham to shorten the route by 4½ miles.
**Or: Turn R** into Tanners Hill, later Old School Lane, and ride for 1 mile. **Turn R** into a lane and soon **bear R** into Tilehurst Lane. Ride up the hill and under the railway bridge before **turning R** at the T-junction into Punchbowl Lane. Climb a little and then sail down the hill for a mile to the A25 on the outskirts of Dorking. **Turn R** onto the cycle track alongside the A25 and follow this for ½ mile to Betchworth Park Golf Course. **Turn R** and onto the pleasant track, Coach Road, for nearly a mile. This skirts the golf course. **Turn L** at the T-junction with the lane to return to Brockham. Then **turn R** to the green.

On the green you could sit at one of the pubs and, whilst resting, admire the view of the pretty cottages with their backdrop of the North Downs. Go to Christ Church along one of the pathways and, keeping it on your right, ride into attractive Wheelers Lane, part of the SCW. In ¾ mile at the T-junction **turn L**, still on the SCW, and ride along this pastoral and tranquil lane to the

next T-junction. **Turn R**, away from the SCW, into Snower Hill for 1⅓ miles to Dawesgreen. There is a chance to pick up speed here with a good hill to sail down.

At the T- junction **turn L** and immediately L again into Flanchford Road, although first you may be visiting the Seven Stars pub. In ⅓ mile you could make a detour to the village of Leigh for the Plough pub and to peep inside St Bartholomew's church. Back on Flanchford Road ride for 1¼ miles then **fork L** down into Clayhall Lane. In ½ mile **turn L** at the start of the houses to climb the hill.

In ½ mile **turn L** onto the Greensand Way, Littleton Lane, which leads to Heathfield Farm. In about ½ mile, as you approach the farm gates, **turn R** into a bridleway, perhaps pushing your bike up the sandy hill. At the top, look out to your left for the Skimmington Castle pub which, with its home-made food, makes an excellent place for lunch. Make your way towards it, even if you are not intending to stop. Then continue down the drive, past the golf course to Flanchford Road. **Turn R** to return to the car park.

## REIGATE HEATH WINDMILL AND ST CROSS CHAPEL

This is said to be the only windmill in the world to have a consecrated chapel. The post mill, which was built in the mid 18th century, has a red-brick roundhouse and a tarred weatherboarded tower. A century later when the mill was no longer working, the roundhouse was converted into a chapel which can seat a congregation of 50. It is a most interesting place, where the four beams of the mill predominate and are just above head height. A working chapel, Evensong is held monthly during the summer months. The key to the chapel can be collected from the golf club next door.

*Buckland village stores*

## BROCKHAM GREEN

Brockham is perhaps one of the most photographed villages in Surrey with its large green surrounded by a variety of attractive house styles. The green was common pasture land for the agricultural community until 1812 but later was used as a cricket pitch. Cricket balls and car windscreens proved to be incompatible so cricket was transferred to the local recreation ground. The village green is now reputed to have one of the largest bonfires and firework displays in England to celebrate Guy Fawkes Night. Christ Church, on the south side of the green, was designed in 1846 by Benjamin Ferrey, biographer and pupil of Augustus Pugin, the foremost architect and designer of the 19th century.

# 13 Bookham, Cobham and Epsom

*23 miles*

This route is unusual and particularly surprising in that it encompasses urban areas to the north of the Surrey Hills, yet a great proportion is on easy rural paths and tracks. Starting at Great Bookham Common and crossing the River Mole to Cobham, ride along quiet roads and bridleways to reach the Commons where one track merges into the next. You will explore Fairmile, Esher, Claygate and Epsom Commons, as well as Horton Park before perhaps taking a break beside the lake at Stamford Green. And besides all that, there are woods galore, Ashtead Park, a nature reserve at Fetcham, and a possible detour to beautiful Painshill Park.

**Maps:** OS Landranger 187 Dorking and Reigate, OS Explorers 146 Dorking, Box Hill and Reigate and 161 London South (GR TQ129557).

**Starting point:** The National Trust's Tunnel car park on Great Bookham Common is a few yards to the east of Bookham station. From the A246, the Leatherhead to Guildford road, turn right into Bookham High Street and the car park is 1 mile ahead to your right.

**By train:** Bookham and Chessington South stations.

**Refreshments:** Café Aromas is in Hollyhedge Road, Cobham, while Chessington South station has a small shop for snacks and at Stamford Green, near Epsom Common, there is the attractive Cricketers pub beside a lake. Watson's bakery in Fetcham serves drinks and snacks.

**The route:** The route snakes back and forth over the A3 mainly on easy bridleways. Although there are some inclines it is a relatively flat route and a good one for families. There are two busy roads to cross, the A244 and the A24.

Ride towards the common and **fork L** along a wide track. Continue your direction across the common following the bridleway to Downside. On a rising lane you go under the M25. Just past a junction at Downside **turn R** by tiny St Michael's chapel. Follow the narrow bridleway through fields towards Cobham Tilt. **Turn R** into the lane.

In ¼ mile **turn L** onto a bridleway at the bend and ride over a planked bridge above the fast flowing River Mole. **Turn L** into Tilt Road and cycle past the Running Mare pub. **Bear L** onto the A245 and ride for ½ mile to Cobham centre, passing the watermill on your left. Painshill Park is ⅓ mile ahead, if you would like to make a detour, but bear in mind that it is

*The nature reserve at Fetcham*

extensive! **Turn R** into Hogshill Lane at the pedestrian lights, perhaps having first visited Café Aromas to your left.

From Hogshill Lane to the woodland car park on Fairmile Common there is an unswerving bridleway, that runs along roads on occasions, in a north-easterly direction, for 2 miles. Do *not* follow bends in the road! Look for a path, which may be narrow or obscured, but is always straight ahead.

From the car park **turn L** into Sandy Lane and, after the bend, **turn L** into a bridleway, SP Esher Common cycle route. **Turn L** at a junction of wide tracks and go over the A3. **Turn R** on the track to a signposted crossways. **Fork half R**, SP Arbrook Common. In a mile, cross the busy A244 to the path opposite.

**Fork R** soon and at a lane, **turn R** and then **L** into a bridleway following logos. In 200 yards **fork R**, leaving the bike trail, and for over a mile follow signs to Claygate. Go under the A3 and, after bends, under a railway bridge, before a delightful ride through woods.

**Turn L** at a T-junction of tracks and go over the A3. **Turn R** into Holroyd Road. In 200 yards **turn L** through posts into a horse ride. The track eventually opens out at a small car park. **Turn R** here along a rising bridleway and go over the A3. Follow the path ahead, later swinging sharply left. **Bear R** into Barwell Lane and ride downwards over the speed ramps.

Cross the A243 and climb Garrison Lane, passing Chessington South station. In a mile **fork R** into Stokesby

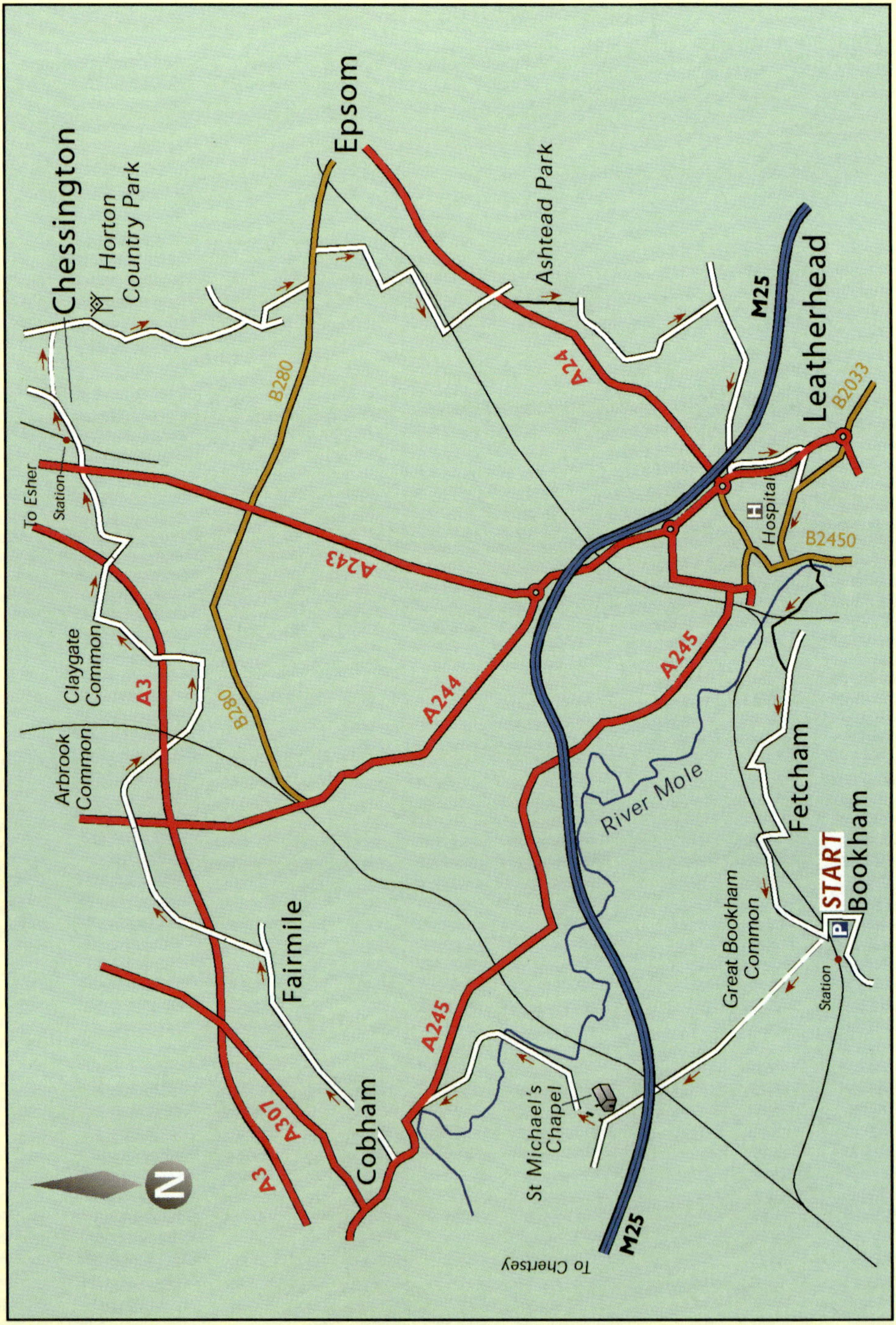

Chessington
Horton Country Park
Epsom
Ashtead Park
Leatherhead
M25
B2033
B280
A24
To Esher
Station
A243
Hospital
B2450
Claygate Common
A3
A244
A245
Arbrook Common
River Mole
Fetcham
START
Bookham
Great Bookham Common
Station
Fairmile
Cobham
A307
St Michael's Chapel
To Chertsey

*The River Mole*

Road, soon cross the grassed oval by shops and sail down Filby Road, stopping near the bottom. **Turn R** into the footpath through Castle Hill Wood to Horton Country Park.

**Turn R** at the main track. **Fork L** in ½ mile. **Turn R** at a T- junction to maintain your southerly direction across tracks and past a totem pole to Horton Lane.

Cross the road obliquely **R** and go into the cycle path. Gradually bearing right, go to the B280. Cross to the shared path and **turn L**. Pass Christ Church and **turn R** into Stamford Green Road. The Cricketers pub is to your left beside the lake, where a heron is often to be seen.

Ride on to a T-junction and **turn R**, and soon into a pathway. **Turn L** at Wells Road and **R** before the railway line into Woodlands Road going on into the track. **Turn L** at the Thames Down Link to cross the railway. Cycle through woods to Craddocks Avenue. **Turn L** and then **R** onto the A24. In ⅓ mile **turn L** through iron gates into Ashtead Park and continue for ½ mile to the City of London Freeman's School.

**Turn R** to Dene Road. In ½ mile, at a sharp right-hand bend, **turn L** to climb Crampshaw Road for ¾ mile. Go into a pathway to your right through woodland for ½ mile to a four-way junction. **Turn R**, SP M25, for 1 mile. **Fork L** into Green Lane and glide down the hill.

**Turn L** onto the pathway and go over the M25. Cycle on the winding path and **turn L** to find the pathway running parallel to the A24. It snakes through the woods for ¾ mile making a good ride. Cross the A24 via the bollard and **turn R** into Headley Road. Continue downwards and over the speed bumps to Leatherhead.

**Turn L** onto Dorking Road and in ¼ mile **turn R** across the River Mole. Don't miss this attractive part of the River Mole, best seen from the bridge. In ¼ mile **turn R** onto the permissive cycleway to Leatherhead Leisure Centre where you **turn R**. At the T- junction **turn R** onto the B2212. Take the first exit at the roundabout and **turn L** into Mill Lane and go under the railway bridge. Shortly, **fork L** to ride beside the lake in the nature reserve.

**Turn R** at Cobham Road and cycle for a mile to Fetcham village. Here there are some refreshment opportunities. **Turn sharp L** by the service station before the railway bridge. Soon **turn R** into Cock Lane and in ½ mile **R** into Kennel Lane. Go onto the narrow bridleway, over the railway and **turn L** onto a track. **Turn R** into The Glade and cycle to Great Bookham Common. **Bear L** back to the car park.

## COBHAM WATERMILL

The small 19th-century watermill, standing on the banks of the River Mole, was restored by a dedicated group of local enthusiasts during the early 1990s and is now the only working watermill in Surrey. The Cobham Mill Preservation Trust has taken over responsibility for the mill which is opened to the public to demonstrate the milling of corn. This is on the second Sunday of each month between April and October, from 2 pm to 5 pm.

## PAINSHILL PARK

Extending to 158 acres, Painshill is said to be one of the finest examples of an 18th-century landscape park. It was created from heathland at the time of the Landscape Movement, by the plantsman and designer, Charles Hamilton. The parkland fell into decay after the Second World War but was bought by Elmbridge Borough Council in 1980. It has been gradually restored to its former glory, under the guiding hand of the Painshill Park Trust. Stretching over hills and valleys, it has a long and tranquil lake, elegant bridges, an enchanting crystal grotto and several follies, including an exotic Turkish tent and a Gothic temple.

14

# Horsley, Box Hill and Ranmore

### *21, with options up to 29½, miles*

This ride offers a route with the opportunity to add some major Surrey highlights. Enjoy the oak woodlands and wetlands of Great Bookham Common, Bocketts – a delightful working family farm – and a superb descent from Norbury Park to Mickleham, whilst Ranmore Common offers splendid southerly views. Make all the detours to see the most stunning panoramas in the North Downs from Box Hill, visit glorious Denbies, the largest vineyard in England, and view the superb National Trust flagship property, Polesden Lacey. The full route is challenging and includes a classic climb up the Zigzag to Box Hill.

**Maps:** OS Landranger 187 Dorking and Reigate, OS Explorers 145 Guildford and Farnham, 146 Dorking, Box Hill and Reigate (GR TQ088525).

**Starting point:** The car park at St Mary the Virgin church between East and West Horsley. From Leatherhead take the A246 in the direction of Guildford. Pass the Ramada Hotel at East Horsley and in ½ mile turn left onto the track before the church.

**By train:** Horsley, Effingham Junction and West Humble stations are all on the route.

**Refreshments:** Bocketts Farm, Leatherhead, serves drinks and light snacks. In Mickleham there is the Running Horses pub whilst on Box Hill there is a National Trust refreshment kiosk. A highlight is Denbies Vineyard restaurant.

**The route:** There are 5 miles of relatively flat and easy off-road riding around Horsley and Great Bookham Common but expect hills even on the core route. You can tailor-make the ride to include: Box Hill 3½ miles return (paragraph 6), Polesden Lacey, 4 miles return, and Denbies, 1 mile return. Be prepared for three busy road crossings: the A246 at Horsley and Leatherhead and the A24 north of Dorking.

Ride from the car park to cross the A246. **Turn R** and soon **turn L** into the second driveway, a bridleway, which goes towards Place Farm and then skirts to the right of it. This is now a paper recycling plant. Keep ahead with the farm to your left. This becomes a pleasant track past fields and woods to the railway. **Turn R** and follow the path to the B2039, the Ockham road. **Turn L** under the bridge by Horsley station. In ⅓ mile **turn R** to climb Drift Road which runs beside the golf course.

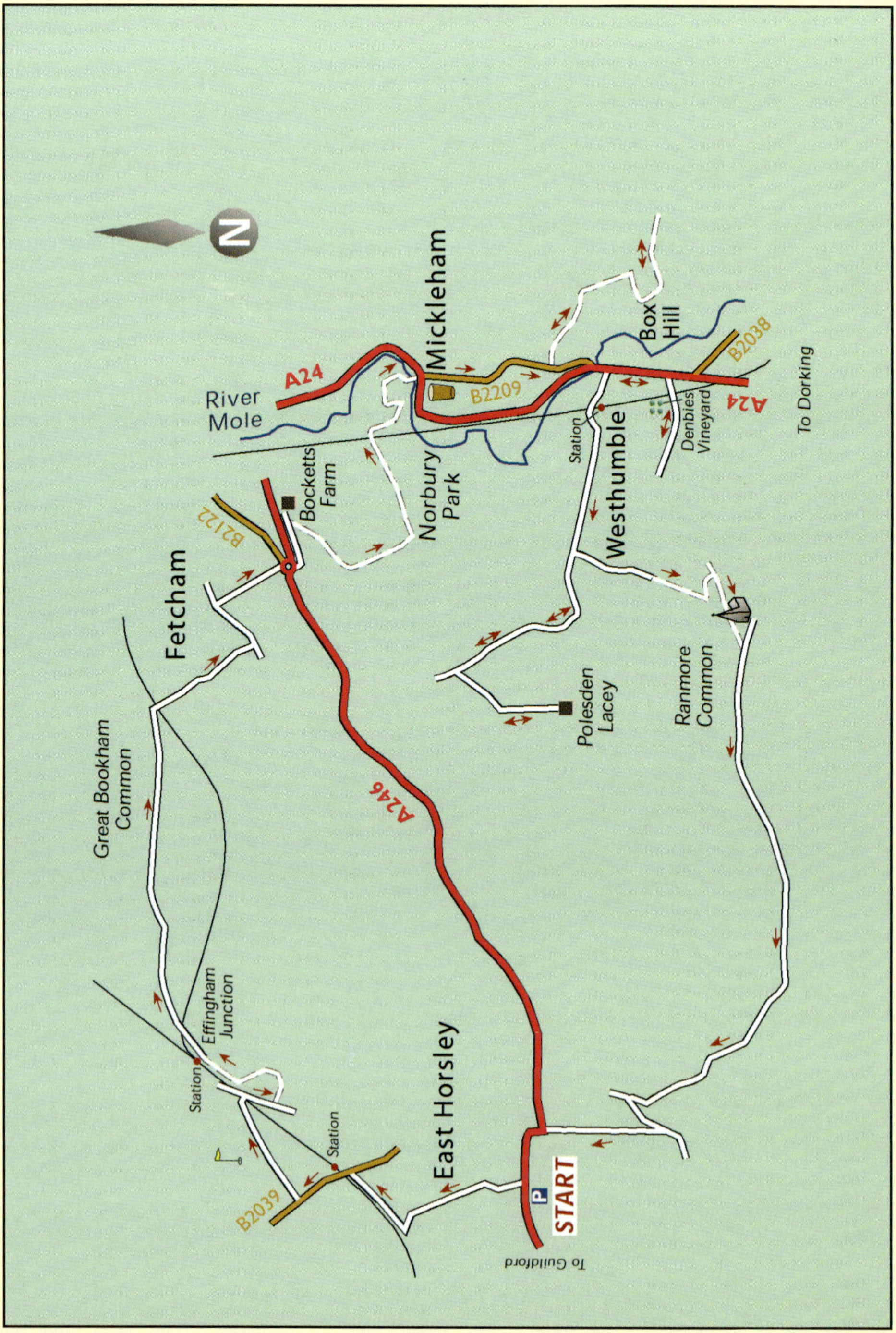

# 14 Horsley, Box Hill and Ranmore

N
Mickleham
River Mole
A24
B2209
Box Hill
B2038
To Dorking
Denbies Vineyard
Station
Westhumble
Norbury Park
Bocketts Farm
B2122
Fetcham
Polesden Lacey
Ranmore Common
A246
Great Bookham Common
Effingham Junction
Station
East Horsley
Station
B2039
P
START
To Guildford

*Looking over Denbies vineyard to Box Hill*

At the T-junction **turn R** over the railway bridge. In about 200 yards **turn L** into Heathway, follow the road round to the right and at the end of the grassed area **turn L** into the bridleway, **forking L** again through woodland. **Turn R** opposite bungalows, to follow signs to Effingham Junction station on the surfaced path. **Turn R** at the station and **L** past the bus shelter through white gates onto a permissive bridleway.

The route lies ahead on bridleways for 2½ miles, gradually bearing to the right. Watch for signposts with blue bridleway arrows making for Great Bookham Common, where there will be two large ponds on your right. Then head in the Fetcham direction and **bear L** to leave the common and go to the Glade, a residential road.

Keeping to the paved road, go over the bridge and sail down the Glade into Fetcham. **Turn R** at the T-junction into Kennel Lane. **Turn L** at the T-junction with Lower Road and go down to the roundabout. **Turn R** at the Ridgeway and climb to **turn R** into the B2122 and cross the Leatherhead bypass to Norbury Park.

Visit Bocketts Farm and enjoy a rest at the café in the barn by **turning L** and riding down the hill into the farm entrance. Upon leaving, **turn L** into a bridleway, just before the car park. Cycle for ½ mile to cross tracks and **turn L**.

Climb the hill for ⅓ mile on the rough track and then **bear L** at a large grassy area. In a further ½ mile, at a junction and clearing, the Norbury Park sawmill is to your right. Keep straight ahead on the paved lane and enjoy the amazing descent with fabulous views to Mickleham Downs and Cherkley Court, Lord Beaverbrook's much-loved retreat. **Turn R** at the base and ride to the A24. Cross over into Mickleham village where there is the Coach and Horses pub. Ignore the detour below to continue the main route.

**Detour to Box Hill: Turn L** in 1 mile to make the classic climb up the Zigzag. At the top there is the National Trust kiosk for snacks, whilst further on is

*On the open road*

the panoramic view from Saloman's memorial towards the South Downs. Return down the Zigzag and **turn L**.

Pass Rykers and the Burford Bridge Hotel on the B2209. **Turn L** onto the cycle path and soon ride beneath the A24 before taking the left-hand slope to the cycle track. **Detour to Denbies Vineyard:** ride on ⅓ mile to the south on the cycle track and **turn R** to the main building; retrace your route. **For the main route: turn R** towards Westhumble station, and in 1¼ miles **turn L** into Ranmore Common Road. **Detour to Polesden Lacey:** by continuing along Chapel Lane. In 1½ miles **turn L** into Polesden Road and continue ½ mile to the house; afterwards return to Ranmore Common Road.

Make the 1-mile climb to Ranmore Common. If you are pushing your bike, you can enjoy attractive fields and shady woodland. The road levels out at the top and you pass the church of St Barnabas, whose spire is a distinctive landmark. **Turn R** at the T-junction. At the National Trust car park, park your bike, go through the gate and walk a few yards to see the wonderful southerly views over Dorking. Then continue on **SCW** over Ranmore Common and Crocknorth Road, over the ups and downs, for 3½ miles. At a T-junction **turn sharp L** and in ⅓ mile **turn R** into Chalk Lane and ride for ¾ mile to the A246. **Turn L** and the church and car park are ½ mile on your left.

### POLESDEN LACEY

The setting is spectacular, with beautiful views from the long terrace over the Surrey Hills. King George VI and Queen Elizabeth chose it as their honeymoon destination. In addition to the Edwardian collections in the house, there are extensive formal and rose gardens together with a farm shop, a gift shop and a restaurant. Leaflets regarding the history can be obtained from the property.

### DENBIES VINEYARD

Denbies is the largest vineyard in England. Tours and wine tasting are available within the winery building, whilst the vineyard train climbs the slopes to offer splendid views of Box Hill. The stylish restaurant in the conservatory atrium has a servery for light meals.

### MICKLEHAM

The Running Horses pub, a restored 17th-century building, was renamed in 1828. This followed a dead heat between two horses, *Colonel* and *Cadland*, in the Derby. The two bars are named after these horses and the inn sign has a picture of each horse, one on either side.

# 15

# Epsom Downs, Walton Heath and Colley Hill

***20 miles***

The highlights of the ride are the spectacular views from both Reigate Hill and Colley Hill, quirky Fanny's Kitchen farm shop, the popular Sportsman pub at Mogador, Mere Pond at Walton on the Hill and glorious and atmospheric Epsom Downs. It is a route of contrasts with high downs, long views, the greens of Walton Heath golf course and the racecourse at Epsom. There is usually a holiday atmosphere on Epsom Downs and you could strike lucky by passing on Derby Day, but find an alternative location to park!

**Maps:** OS Landranger 187 Dorking and Reigate, OS Explorer 146 Dorking, Box Hill and Reigate (GR TQ220587).

**Starting point:** Park in the car park on Grand Stand Road, Epsom Downs, close to the roundabout and grandstand.

**By train:** Tattenham Corner station is close by the start of the route.

**Refreshments:** On Epsom Downs there is the Rubbing House with its Downs views, or the Derby Arms across the road. In Walton on the Hill there is Café Chocolat and the Fox and Hounds and at Reigate Hill there is a National Trust kiosk. There is also Fanny's Kitchen farm shop at Merstham and the excellent Sportsman at Mogador.

**The route:** Half of the route is off-road on paths and tracks whilst the rest is on quiet roads, except for Gatton Bottom but you will cover the ground fast. The map shows an alternative route from the B2032 to Langley Vale, near Epsom Downs, which substitutes 1¾ miles of bridleways, which may be affected in damp conditions, with roads.

Do give plenty of space when you encounter young racehorses around the Epsom Downs area. They are beautiful creatures but highly strung, and often very nervous of bicycles.

**Turn R** out of the car park and take the second exit at the roundabout. At the pedestrian lights, opposite Derby Stables, **turn L** onto the path. Cross the racecourse to the Rubbing House.

**Turn half L** along the surfaced switchback, maintaining a southerly direction for 1 mile. Cross the racecourse again, soon cross a track and go ahead onto a grass-covered path.

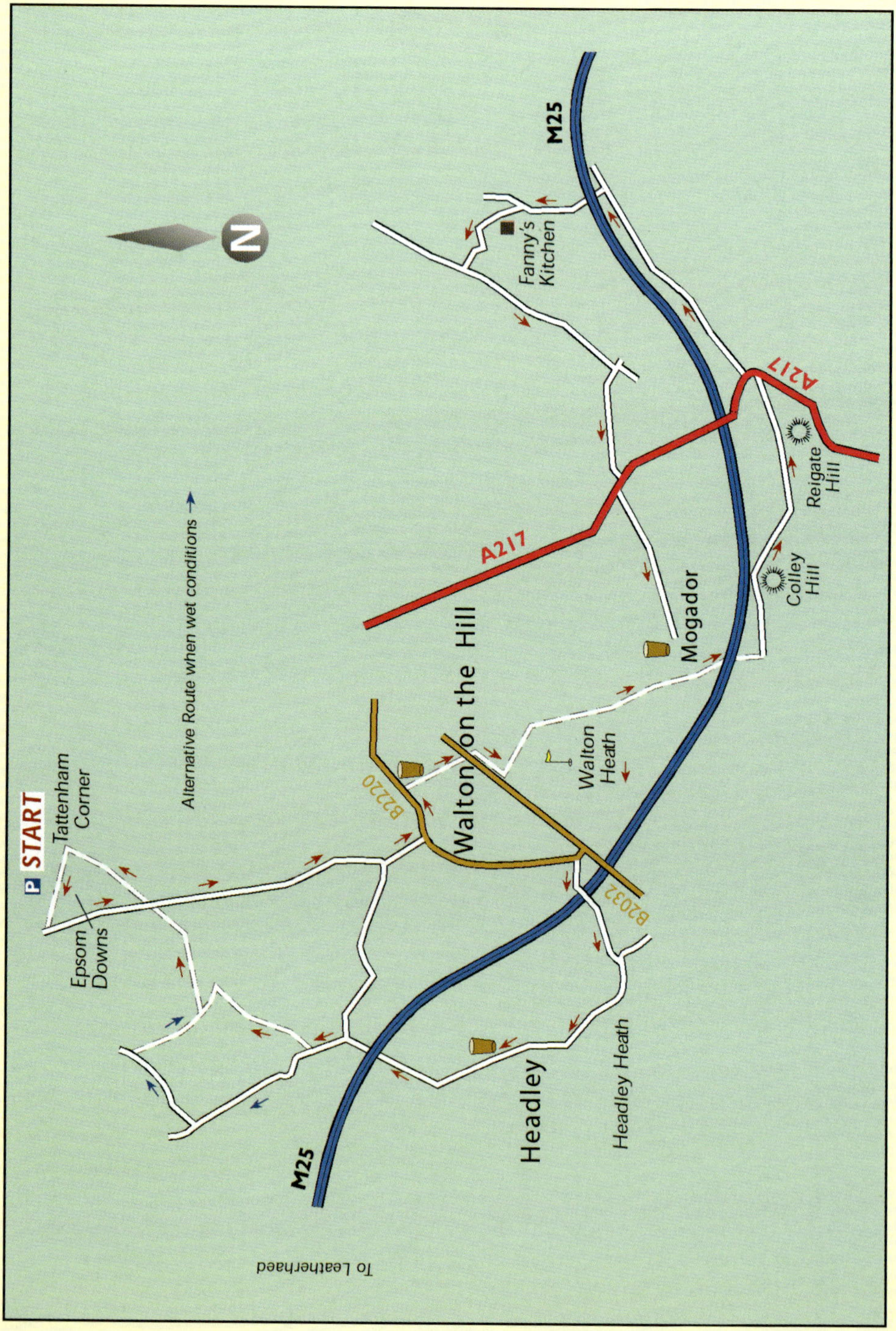

# 15 Epsom Downs, Walton Heath and Colley Hill

*The impressive Inglis monument atop Colley Hill*

Descend gradually from Epsom to Walton Downs and into Ebbisham Lane. The spire of Headley church is to your right.

Ride for 1½ miles along the lane towards Walton on the Hill, **bearing L** after a mile. At the major crossroads **turn L** and cycle through the village, but first you would do well to look inside St Peter's church with its fine stained-glass windows. The Fox and Hounds is on your left and in ⅓ mile there is the opportunity to linger at Café Chocolat overlooking Mere pond.

**Turn R** into Deans Lane. Soon take a bridleway on your left, keeping roughly parallel to the residential area, and cycle ¼ mile to cross the B2032. **Turn R** and soon **L** onto a path bordering Walton Heath golf course and Banstead Heath. In about ¼ mile, at a marker post, **bear half R** in a roughly southerly direction to continue on the bridleway, ignoring the grassland ahead. In a mile, keep ahead at the signposted crosspaths.

Ride for ⅓ mile and **turn R** over the M25. Keeping to the blue bridleway arrows, in ⅕ mile **turn L** into the North Downs Way and cycle for 1½ miles. This is one of the most scenic spots in the Surrey Hills. Pass Colley Hill and on Reigate Hill find a seat to soak up the glorious views. The rotunda is ahead. Next is the National Trust car park where you may decide to patronize the kiosk and rest with a drink.

Cross the car park and **turn L** at the road. Shortly **turn R** and sail down the hill for 1¼ miles to Gatton Bottom. Watch for a brown sign indicating Fanny's Kitchen farm shop. **Turn L** under the M25. Climb the hill and in ½ mile the farm shop is on your left.

Browse in this delightfully quirky place, then go to the rear gate and follow the bridleway. This leads through fields past Park Farm and eventually to the road.

**Turn L** and cycle for a mile to the crossroads. **Turn R** into Babylon Lane. At the A217 go to the pedestrian lights and cross the dual carriageway into Stubbs Lane and ride for over ¾ mile to Mogador. Perhaps detour **R** for ¼ mile to visit the popular Sportsman pub. Otherwise go ahead for 1¼ miles along the wooded bridleway (ignore the private driveway) to a fine ride across Walton Heath golf course to the B2032.

Cross into the B2220 and soon **turn L** into Sturts Lane. Stick to the bridleway for 1¾ miles to Headley Heath, riding over the M25. (Ignore inviting footpaths and tracks and ¼ mile from the M25, take the bridleway that veers right.) At Headley Heath **turn R** to sail down the hill and past the Cock Inn and Headley church. Soon the SCW joins from the left and it is about ⅕ mile before you **turn R** into Hurst Lane and under the M25.

Go ahead into Walton Road and ⅓ mile after the M25 underpass **turn R** into the NCN22, the bridleway, Sheep Walk. At the end of the track **bear L** round the bend. Ignoring the right-hand paths, continue for 200 yards. **Turn R** on the NCN22 up the narrow path to cross the gallop into a lane. Bending left and then right before a cottage, the track straightens and eventually crosses the southern part of the racecourse.

Continue on the NCN22 to Tattenham Corner. This is an exhilarating ride, high on the Downs. **Turn L** into the track just before the northern section of the racecourse. Either ride for ½ mile to visit the Rubbing House ahead or, **turn R** in ⅓ mile, immediately before the grandstand, to use the underpass footpath. Walk your bike to the road and make your way across to the car park.

## EPSOM DOWNS

The Downs have an atmosphere all of their own. From the notice warning that racehorses exercise in the mornings, to the towering grandstand on the skyline, there is a zing in the air. This is the place where the Derby has been held since 1780, one of the toughest races open to three-year-old thoroughbred colts and fillies. Cycle here during the first week of June, Derby Week, and the Downs will be covered with all manner of people – bookmakers, jockeys, trainers and those racegoers who just want to watch – and there is a funfair and the smells of hot food. Look for the Gherkin building in central London from Tattenham Corner and for Windsor Castle and St Paul's Cathedral from the grandstand.

## FANNY'S KITCHEN

This is a farm shop with a difference that needs to be experienced. As well as a great variety of locally sourced produce, Fanny has an extraordinary array of marmalades. It is said that there are more varieties stocked than at Fortnum and Mason's, and the annual marmalade competition attracts over a hundred entries. Outside there are also some fantastic pieces to discover such as the gartered leg! Fanny has been in business for 34 years, having started by selling potatoes and eggs at her gate, but now wins awards for being the best retailer of the year in Redhill.

16

# Woldingham, Warlingham and Chelsham

*18 miles*

Offering some beautiful and varied countryside with panoramic views from the North Downs, this ride is the more surprising given its proximity to Croydon. Pause for a drink at Botley Farmhouse, cross the Kent border to Biggin Hill and wend your way to Fickleshole and the White Bear, a characterful 16th-century pub. Ride off-road along the Sustrans Cycle Route, the NCN21, to cut through miles of woodland and drop down towards the greens of Woldingham golf course. Treat yourself at the Dene coffee shop with its flower-filled gardens before riding back along a delightful hidden valley past Woldingham School.

**Maps:** OS Landranger 187 Dorking and Reigate, or OS Explorers 146 Dorking, Box Hill and Reigate and 147 Sevenoaks and Tonbridge (GR TQ373540).

**Starting point:** The small car park at South Hawke, Gangers Hill, Woldingham. Exit the M25 at junction 6. Take the A22 towards Godstone, then the third exit at the roundabout onto the A25. Soon turn right into Flower Lane and the woodland car park is about 2 miles on the left. If the car park is full, follow the route in paragraph 1 for 1 mile to alternative parking.

**By train:** Woldingham station.

**Refreshments:** Botley Farm House, the Dene Coffee Shop at Knights Garden Centre, Woldingham, and the White Bear at Fickleshole. Tea and cakes are available for small numbers at St Mary's church, Tatsfield, on Sundays 3 pm to 5 pm, Easter to September.

**The route:** The first half is on-road, whilst the second half is mainly off-road on the NCN21 cycle route. This is hilly country with good descents. The first part of the return leg slopes gently downwards but expect a good challenging hill back to the car park at the end.

**Turn L** out of the car park and ride up to the T-junction. **Turn R** and cycle for 1¾ miles to the B269 at Botley Hill, passing a large car park with panoramic views. Consider a 200-yard detour left to Botley Hill Farmhouse and an opportunity to sit back and admire a splendid downs outlook. Otherwise **turn R** onto the B269 and in a few yards take the first exit into the B2024 SP Westerham.

*The signposted NCN21 at Woldingham*

In just over a mile, as you go down the hill, **turn L** into a narrow lane SP Tatsfield. Climb the hill and St Mary's church is on your left. Wander into the churchyard where, at 790 ft, you can see more stunning views of the North Downs.

Continue straight ahead for 1¾ miles as you ride up, and then down, steep Ricketts Hill to the T-junction at Biggin Hill. **Turn R** and immediately **L** into Sunningvale Avenue. In ½ mile **turn L** at the roundabout into Norheads Lane and soon **turn L** again, as the lane turns away from the major road. Climb the steep hill. Go through a barrier and the lane becomes a track which you follow for just over a mile across the top of the downs. In less than ¾ mile, just past a footpath sign, look to your right and, on a clear day, through a gap in the trees, you should catch a glimpse of Canary Wharf and the Gherkin.

**Turn R** at the end of the track into the delightfully rural Beddlestead Lane where you have a good descent followed by a climb to the top of the hill. **Turn R** at the crossroads and ride for 1¼ miles along the ridge which is also the Kent/Surrey border. In ¾ mile **turn first L** into Blackman's Lane. *Shortly you will see the sign for the NCN21 route which you follow for the next 7¼ miles – look for the blue signs with the red number. Skip to the last paragraph or follow the detailed route below.*

**In detail:** In Fickleshole you may decide to rest at the characterful 16th-century White Bear Inn. The large white polar bear outside makes it

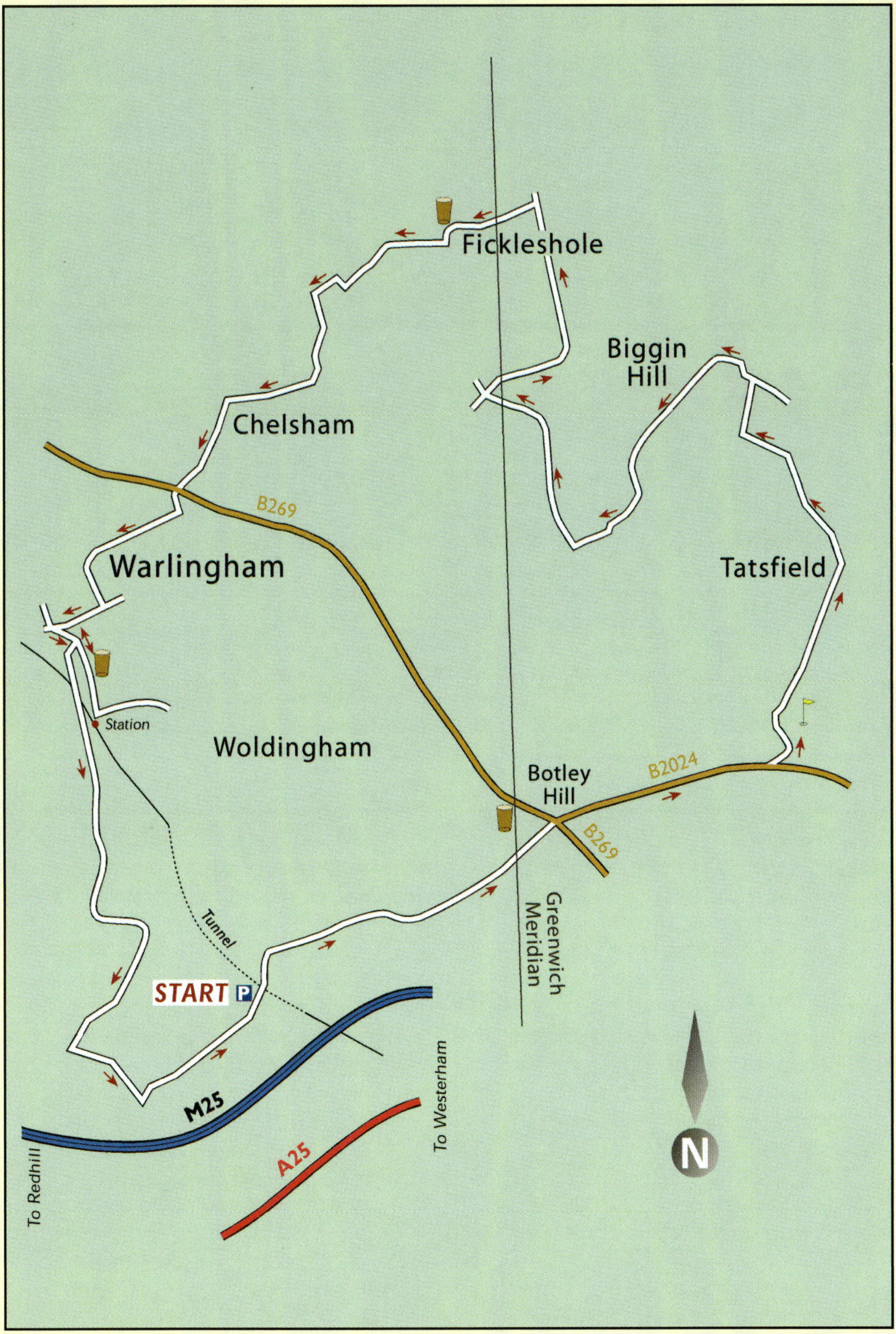

Fickleshole
Biggin Hill
Chelsham
B269
Warlingham
Tatsfield
Station
Woldingham
Botley Hill
B2024
B269
Greenwich Meridian
Tunnel
START P
M25
To Westerham
A25
To Redhill
N

*The welcoming coffee shop at Knights Garden Centre*

hard to miss! In 200 yards, **turn R** into the signed NCN21, a track to a metal gate where the path switchbacks. In ¾ mile **turn R** at a T-junction into a lane. In a few yards **turn L** into the bridleway and ride through Holt Wood.

**Turn R** at the T-junction into Church Lane. (Here the blue NCN21 direction sign is currently missing). Cycle for ½ mile. **Bear L** into the major Chelsham Common Road before **turning L** in a few yards opposite Kennel Farm, into the pathway NCN21. Ride along the path for ½ mile to the Limpsfield Road, the B269.

Cross straight over into High Lane. In 200 yards **turn R** into the bridleway, known as Halliloo Plantation. Here there are some good views through gaps in the hedge to the greens as you ride down to Woldingham golf course. Pass the club house and, just before reaching the road, **turn R** along the parallel path for ⅕ mile. At a narrow gate on your left, cross the road and, following NCN21, go down to the Woldingham road. Cross straight over into the bridleway opposite, or first detour by **turning L** for a few yards to visit the Dene Coffee Shop at Knights Garden Centre, set in beautiful gardens. The tea and cakes are delicious too!

Back on NCN21, cycle the ¼ mile to the top of the path and **turn L** into Woldingham School drive. This is a

beautiful scenic and pastoral section which rises gently. Pedal nearly 1½ miles to the school buildings and past them to East Lodge, where you **bear R** through wrought-iron gates along a further mile of rising driveway through glorious countryside.

**Bear L** at the barrier, away from the NCN21, and follow the trackway, which has ramps, for ⅓ mile to Gangers Hill. **Turn L** into Gangers Hill Road and climb for a mile up the wooded lane back to the car park.

## ST MARY'S CHURCH, TATSFIELD

St Mary's church is more than 780 ft above sea level and is reputed to be the highest church in Surrey. From the churchyard there are quite exceptional views across the Weald: to the south-east is Sevenoaks, to the south Limpsfield and to the south-west you can see the spire of Titsey church and Oxted. Following the murder of Thomas à Becket in 1170, St Mary's was probably established as a chapel of ease for pilgrims on the nearby Pilgrims' Way between Winchester and Canterbury. Unusually, it is now used for both Anglican and Roman Catholic services.

## THE WHITE BEAR, FICKLESHOLE

The White Bear is a Grade II listed building which dates from the 16th century but has been extended over the years by adding the neighbouring row of artisans' cottages. As a consequence it is a most attractive rambling pub with separated rooms, varying floor levels and two inglenooks. Unsurprisingly, given its age, there are said to be two resident ghosts. The white bear is supposed to have originated from Piccadilly Circus or perhaps replaced an earlier wooden design. There is also the story that it narrowly escaped being 'kidnapped' by Polish pilots from Biggin Hill at the end of the Second World War. However authentic the stories, it is a pub well worth visiting for its cosy atmosphere and good food.

17

# South Merstham, Outwood and Lingfield

### *33 miles, or 14½ miles*

Just to the south of the Surrey Hills area, the route follows a national cycle network route through a nature reserve, past urban Redhill and over rural countryside, offering an insight into the diversity of the area. View the working mill at Outwood and explore attractive Lingfield, with its timbered houses. Climb Tilburstow Hill and see glimpses of the South Downs from the bridleway, before enjoying a swift descent to picturesque Bletchingley. Lamington's unique tea shop may be open where you can sample Paul's delicious home-made cakes.

**Maps:** OS Landranger 187 Dorking and Reigate, and OS Explorer 146 Dorking, Box Hill and Reigate (GR TQ300517).

**Starting point:** The car park at Mercers Country Park, South Merstham. From Redhill take the A25 in the direction of Godstone. Turn left in a mile and in ¾ mile, turn right, following the brown signs.

**By train:** Redhill and Earlswood stations. Lingfield station is less than ½ mile away.

**Refreshments:** The Inn on the Pond, Nutfield Marsh, Poppins café at Salfords for their popular breakfast, Joyce's With Best Wishes for light lunches and teas in Lingfield, the Brickmakers' Arms, Crowhurst and Lamington's tea rooms in Bletchingley. The route has pubs in the villages, as well as the Fox and Hounds at the base of Tilburstow Hill.

**The route:** is mostly on easy paths, using the NCN21, and minor roads. The B2028 near Lingfield is a busier section and you cross the A22 and A25. There are definite ups and downs but only Tilburstow Hill presents a real challenge.

From Mercers Country Park **turn L** past fields and in ⅓ mile **turn R** by a blue NCN21 sign. Follow the NCN signs, SP Redhill and Horley, for the next 5½ miles to the Salfords area. Skip to paragraph 5, or see the detailed route below.

**In detail:** Pass the Inn on the Pond and the cricket green and go into the lane. **Turn R** into Cormongers Lane and after 150 yards **turn L** into a path past a barrier and logs. Go through the Moors Nature Reserve and enter the outskirts of Redhill. **Turn R** at the

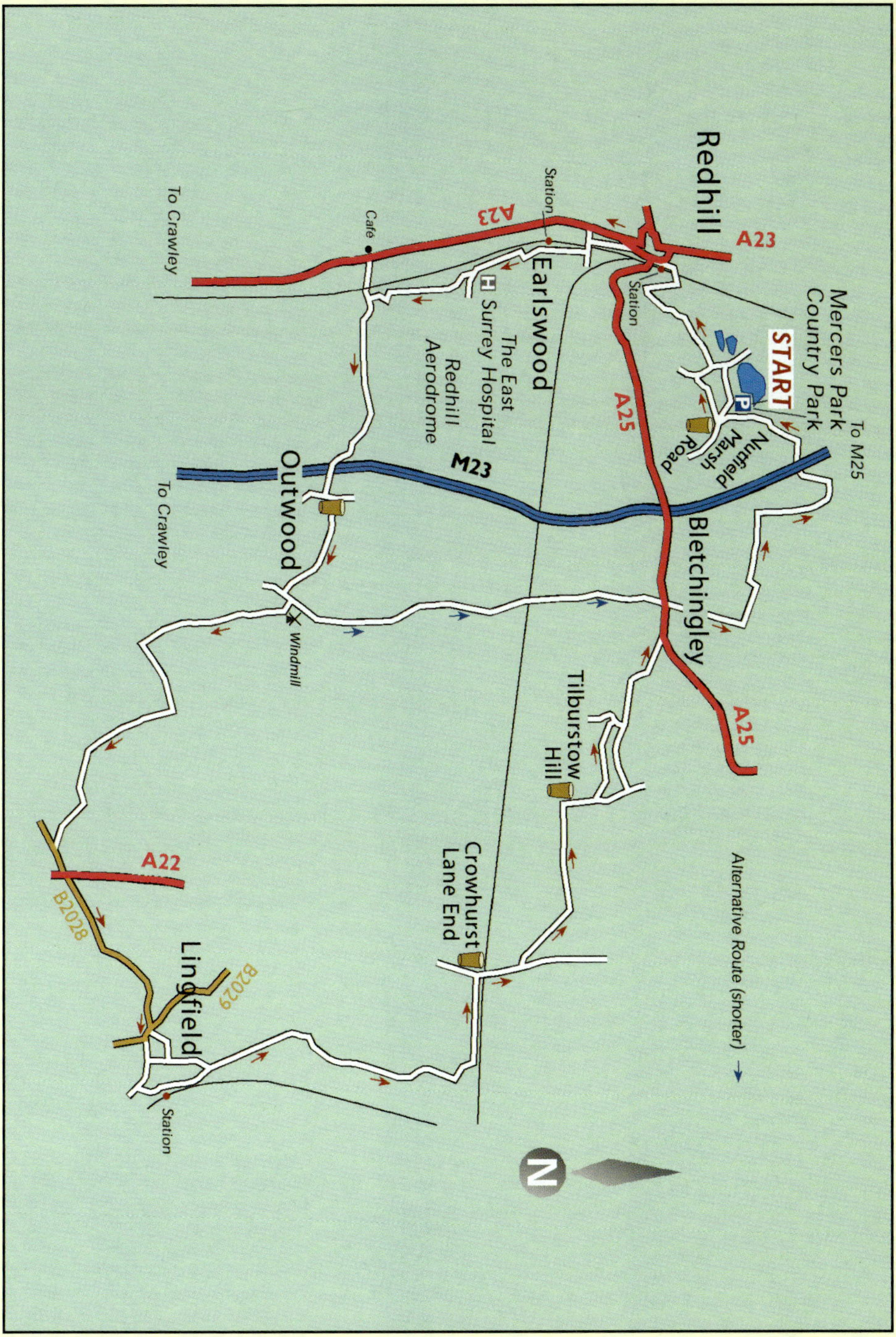
Redhill
A23
A23
Station
Mercers Park
Country Park
START
P
To M25
Nuffield
Marsh
Road
Station
Earlswood
H
The East
Surrey Hospital
Redhill
Aerodrome
Café
To Crawley
A25
M23
Outwood
To Crawley
Bletchingley
Windmill
Tilburstow
Hill
A25
Crowhurst
Lane End
Alternative Route (shorter)
A22
B2028
Lingfield
B2029
Station
N

*The 18th-century Cage in Lingfield*

traffic lights and go under the railway bridge.

**Turn L** onto the A23 and soon go into the cycle track for ¼ mile. After the BP garage **turn L** into Brook Road and then **L** into Hooley Lane and under the railway bridge. **Turn R** into Earlsbrook Road and follow Prince's Road before **turning R** into Arch Road to the end. Pedal on through woods and past fields.

Cross the road, by the crossing, at East Surrey Hospital roundabout and go into a rough track and soon into a housing estate. Watch for a **R turn**, uphill, into Yeoman Way. **Turn R** at the top and soon **L** opposite a newsagents. In ½ mile **turn R** at Dean Farm.

At Salfords you can detour 1½ miles **R** to Poppins across the A23. For the route, **turn L** leaving the NCN, and ride 1½ miles going over the M23.

**Turn L** in ¼ mile at the T-junction, passing the Dog and Duck. Shortly **turn R** past Outwood church and Outwood Common. Set back from the road is a butcher's shop which provides locally sourced meat and poultry and delicious home-made pies and pasties. You can even order a hog roast for your party! **Bear L** and **L** again towards Outwood windmill, the oldest working mill in Britain.

**To shorten the route to 14½ miles:** keep Outwood Mill to your right and ride north to Bletchingley. Skip to the end of paragraph 9 to cross the A25 into Church Lane. **For the main route:** **turn R** by the mill and soon R into a public byway for 1⅓ miles to the T-junction. **Turn L**, and in ½ mile **R** into Bones Lane. Ride for 2 miles and **turn L** into the B2028 to pass the Mormon church. At the roundabout take the second exit, ahead, towards Lingfield, 1½ miles distant.

Outwood post mill

**Turn R** at the Lingfield roundabout and **bear L** into the High Street. On the right is Joyce's With Best Wishes where you can browse at the gifts and goodies whilst you await your order. Ask about parking your bike at the rear.

Still on the B2028, you descend and **turn L** into Church Road. Soon, on your left, is an attractive area where there are fine timber-framed houses and the church of St Peter and St Paul. Ride for ½ mile down the hill and **turn L** into Crowhurst Road. Keep ahead for 3½ miles at the off-set crossroads towards Crowhurst Lane End. **Turn R** under the railway bridge by the Brickmakers' Arms.

In ⅓ mile **turn L** into Miles Lane before crossing the busy A22 into Hart's Lane. At Tilburstow Hill **turn R**, perhaps stopping at the Fox and Hounds. In ⅓ mile **turn L** into the Greensand Way which follows the contour, with glimpses of the South Downs. In ¾ mile, **turn R** to Rabies Heath Road. **Turn L** and sail down the hill to the A25. Cross over into the service road to the **L** and push your bike on the pavement. **Turn R** into Church Lane to pass Bletchingley golf course or cross to Lamington's tea rooms.

In a mile, at the T-junction, ***follow NCN21 signs for 4¼ miles*. In detail: turn L**, and shortly **R** by a concealed sign, to pass a barn. In ½ mile **turn R** at a lane, and head north towards the M25. Climb a slope by the motorway and **bend left**, descending to a lane. At the T-junction **turn R** under the M23. Climb for ¼ mile, go through a gate signed 'NCN' and follow the path for a mile past Spynes Mere Nature Reserve to Nutfield Marsh Road.

**Turn R** and in ⅓ mile **turn R** back through the gates of the country park.

## LINGFIELD

Lingfield is well known for its racecourse, Lingfield Park, which was opened in 1890 and is reputed to be one of the most attractive in the country. Now it is especially popular as it has an all-weather track allowing events to take place throughout the year. Leading to the southern gate of St Peter and St Paul's churchyard is a corner where there are beautiful half-timbered 15th- and 16th-century houses to the west side and 17th- and 18th-century houses to the east. The 15th-century church is magnificent too and has, for example, tip-up seats in the choir stalls which can be lifted to expose carved misericords beneath. Next to the village pond and beside a hollow oak is St Peter's Cross. This was built in 1473 to mark the boundary between the two manors, Puttenden and Billeshurst. Attached is an 18th-century cell, The Cage, built to lock up petty offenders, particularly poachers, but there is a tale of a dramatic escape when friends lifted away the roof.

## OUTWOOD

National Trust-owned Outwood Common consists of around 2,000 acres of beautiful woodland and is a popular area for walking. The big attraction of Outwood, however, is its windmill with its 60-ft pair of sails. It is a post mill dating back to 1665 which makes it one of the oldest working mills in Britain. Unfortunately the mill is closed at the time of writing but when it reopens visitors can view the mill at work.

# 18

# Limpsfield, Titsey and The Chart

## *13½ miles*

This is a beautiful area on the Surrey/Kent border. Although the route runs across the M25 and the A25, you ride upon quiet lanes, often with spectacular views, interspersed with short sections of delightful off-road riding. Enjoy an easy and beautiful woodland path, pedal along the Greensand Way with downland views and explore the small and picturesque village of Limpsfield. A short detour allows a visit to Titsey Park, one of the oldest surviving historic estates in Surrey. The Chart lies on the Greensand Ridge and is an area where magnificent beech trees predominate and where the ground is carpeted with bluebells in spring.

**Maps:** OS Landranger 187 Dorking and Reigate, OS Explorer 145 Dorking, Box Hill and Reigate (GR TQ418522).

**Starting point:** Ridlands Grove, a free National Trust car park. From the A25, travelling east from Redhill to Sevenoaks, turn right onto the B269 at Limpsfield. Turn left in ½ mile and the car park is soon on your left.

**By train:** Hurst Green station is ½ mile from the route. Go into Greenhurst Lane, turn right into Hurst Green and left into Tanhouse Lane. Start the ride at paragraph 6.

**Refreshments:** The Grasshopper Inn is 1½ miles from the start on the A25, between Limpsfield and Westerham. The Bull at Limpsfield and the Royal Oak Inn at Staffhurst Wood are a few yards from the route.

**The route:** There are hills, but apart from the last one they are not long and there is a feeling of more downhill than up! There are a couple of short stretches of easy off-road riding. The A25 is crossed twice and there is about a mile on the B269, otherwise the route is quiet.

**Turn L** from the car park and, after passing through the village of The Chart, enjoy well over a mile of downhill through beechwoods. The Grasshopper Inn, just the other side of the A25, dates back to the 12th century and offers an attractive and interesting break. Cycle to the far end of the car park and **turn L** up Clacket Lane, pedalling for 1½ miles. This is a beautiful rural lane with the banks lined by bluebells and stitchwort in spring. It is the more surprising to see the M25 and Clacket Lane Services appear below. The lane rises gradually to the Pilgrims' Way.

**Turn L** for an exhilarating downhill

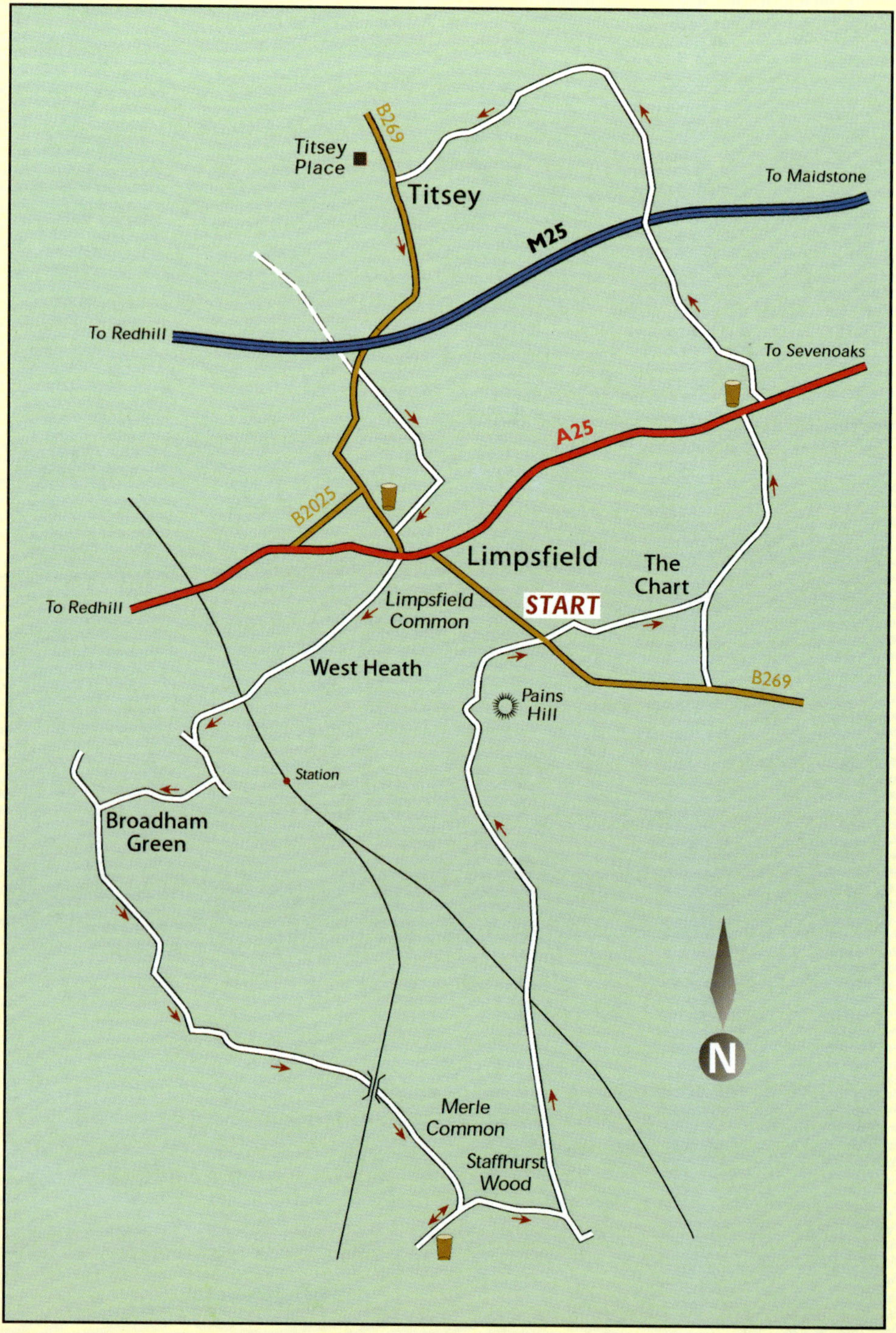

Titsey Place
B269
Titsey
To Maidstone
M25
To Redhill
To Sevenoaks
A25
B2025
Limpsfield
The Chart
To Redhill
Limpsfield Common
START
West Heath
B269
Pains Hill
Station
Broadham Green
N
Merle Common
Staffhurst Wood

*On the Pilgrims' Way between Clacket Lane and Titsey*

between fields with glorious distant views. Soon you reach the hamlet of Titsey with the church of St James. The grounds of Titsey Place lie opposite, although there is no public access here. **Turn L** into the B269. There is a downhill run for ½ mile before going under the M25. Soon there are bridleways on both sides of the road.

To detour to Titsey Place from here, **turn R** into the bridleway to take the ½ mile long rough track to the entrance. For the main route, **turn L** into the lane and pedal up the hill for ½ mile passing some attractive houses on the way. Go ahead into the woods away from the lane, as it bends sharply to the right, and then in a few yards **turn R**, to follow the bridleway down into Limpsfield.

Detour to the **R** if you wish to visit the village of Limpsfield and the 16th-century coaching inn, the Bull in the High Street; from Limpsfield High Street take Bluehouse Lane and then Water Lane to the entrance of Titsey Place. Otherwise, **turn L** and ride up to the traffic lights, moving to the right-hand lane.

Cross the A25 and cycle straight up the hill. **Turn R** into the lane, part of the Greensand Way. There are now 2 miles of particularly enjoyable cycling. When the lane bends to the right, keep straight ahead, across West Heath, and follow the pathway in the open area. Descend to crossroads and go into Icehouse Wood. Sail down the hill and at the bottom **turn R** and then immediately **L** into Woodhurst Lane.

Very soon, **turn R** into Tanhouse Lane. The Haycutter is soon on your left. **Turn L** at the T-junction and ride for ¼ mile past attractive Broadham Green. **Turn L**, as the major road swings right, and ride for ½ mile. You are on the SCW and heading for Merle Common. **Turn L** and continue along Pope's Lane, later becoming Merle Common Road, and climb through the village to pass through beech woods. **Turn R** onto Red Lane.

Consider a detour to visit the Royal Oak Inn by soon **forking R** and the inn is ¼ mile on the left. This is a popular refurbished pub where you can sit outside on the peaceful boarded balcony. Otherwise, **fork L** into Dwelly

*The 12th-century Grasshopper Inn*

Lane and immediately **turn L** into Staffhurst Wood Road. The wood is a Site of Special Scientific Interest and was once a royal hunting forest.

**Turn L** at the T-junction and follow the lane for 2⅓ miles as it crosses the railway line and passes Whitegates Farm. The SCC veers left at Short Lane but keep ahead and climb up Pains Hill. This is a steep one, right at the end of the ride. **Bear R** at Chapel Road near the top, cross over the B269 and into Ridlands Lane. The car park is shortly to your left.

## LIMPSFIELD CHART

This area spreads across the greensand ridge from south-east of Oxted to the Kent border. Predominantly woodland, it is well known for offering excellent paths for riding and walking and is spectacular in spring with its beech woods and carpets of bluebells. Some 240 acres of the common were donated to the National Trust in 1972 by Major Richard Leveson Gower who owned Titsey Place nearby. In Domesday times, stone used to be quarried on the common and in the 12th to 14th centuries stoneware was made in kilns, followed by brickworks in the 19th century. A claim to fame is that in 1895, Major Baden Powell, brother of the founder of the Scout movement, is said to have tried flying from the common with his patented 'Levitor' man-lifting kite.

## TITSEY PARK AND THE HAMLET OF TITSEY

Titsey Place was bought by Sir John Gresham in the 16th century and passed to succeeding generations of Greshams until the female line, the Leveson Gowers, inherited in the early 19th century. It remained in the family until there was just Thomas, a bachelor, who died in 1992. He had set up the Titsey Foundation, a charitable trust, to ensure the estate would be preserved for the public benefit. The house and gardens are open on Wednesdays and Sundays between May and September. Titsey itself is a hamlet lying outside the estate and consists of some cottages and the 19th-century St James' church, a replacement for the demolished Titsey Place church. There are monuments inside the church to the Greshams and Leveson Gowers.

# Windsor Great Park and Virginia Water

## *14 or 10 miles*

This ride is to the north of the Surrey Hills area and is partly in Surrey and partly in Berkshire. It is included because it offers an easy, safe ride for families in the glorious setting of the Crown Estate of Windsor Great Park. It follows the banks of the extensive lake of Virginia Water and there are superlative views of Windsor Castle down the Long Walk from the vantage point of Snow Hill, as well as from Queen Anne's Ride. Admire the equestrian statue of the Queen, or the Copper Horse with George III astride, marvel at the 100 ft high totem pole from British Columbia or the ornamental ruins transported from the site of Leptis Magna near Tripoli. Pause for a delicious lunch at the impressive Savill Gardens building, perhaps browse in the shop or view the gallery in the conservatory. Here there is something for everyone.

**Maps:** OS Explorer 160 Windsor, Weybridge and Bracknell, and ask for a 'Cycling in Windsor Park' leaflet from the village store in Windsor Great Park (GR SU964750).

**Starting point:** The car park by Queen Anne's Gate, Windsor Great Park. Take the A332 on the southern outskirts of Windsor in the direction of Ascot. The car park is just over ½ mile on the right at the start of the park.

**By train:** Both Windsor and Virginia Water stations are about 1½ miles from the route.

**Refreshments:** The post office at the Village in Windsor Great Park sells drinks, rolls and ice creams. The Savill Gardens café offers an excellent variety of hot and cold food, or try the Fox and Hounds pub at Bishopsgate, just outside the park boundary.

**The route:** After the initial off-road section the ride is on surfaced park roads where there is a minimum of traffic and hills. There is a mile, starting near Ascot Gate and ending at Blacknest Gate, where you should push your bike as it is a horse-ride, or leave the park and use the B383, which adds ½ mile. The Virginia Water to Savill Garden section is a beautiful path to ride but becomes busy with pedestrians on weekends and holidays. The Windsor Park cycling map shows alternatives, but they will have some hills!

For the 10-mile alternative, park by the toucan crossing on the A332 and start at paragraph 2.

# 19 Windsor Great Park and Virginia Water

*The totem pole in Windsor Great Park was a gift to the Queen from the people of British Columbia.*

From the car park go through the posts onto the NCN4. After ¼ mile **turn L** up the short slope and at a junction of paths go straight ahead. Continue on past fields and woods to the toucan crossing on the A322.

Cross over at Ranger's Gate and ride up the incline to go ahead at the crossroads and over the brow of the hill. Make a detour by **turning L**, SP Village, for a drink, a snack, or to pick up a 'Cycling in Windsor Park' leaflet. The Post Office and Village Store has a tea garden where you may see swans and cygnets wandering in the road.

Back on the route go past the Isle of Wight Pond and on to Sandpit Gate where the road **bears L**. Soon, at the highest point on Queen Anne's Ride, there is the magnificent Golden Jubilee bronze equestrian statue by Philip Jackson, depicting Queen Elizabeth II on horseback. Distant views to Windsor Castle along the Ride and the Long Walk are spectacular.

At a fork, **turn R** and **R** again into Duke's Lane for a gentle, downward sloping ride past fields and mature trees. Just as the road rises:
**Either: Turn L** into the track, if you are prepared to push your bike for a mile to Blacknest Gate. Cross into a pathway keeping the gate to your right.
**Or:** to remain in the saddle, ride an extra ½ mile and go outside the Park by riding through Prince Consort's Gate. Pedal down the drive and out through Ascot Gate, **turning L** into the B383. In ⅔ mile **turn L** into Mill Lane and, in ¾ mile, **turn L** into the Park through Blacknest Gate. **Turn R** into a pathway.

Pass a kiosk and **bear L** with the tarmac pathway along the southerly banks of Virginia Water and the Obelisk Pond. It is about 3 miles to the Savill Gardens. This is a beautiful meander and there is plenty of interest to enjoy on the way such as Virginia Water itself, the cascade, Leptis Magna, the Roman ruin, and the British Columbian totem pole. At the impressive Savill Garden

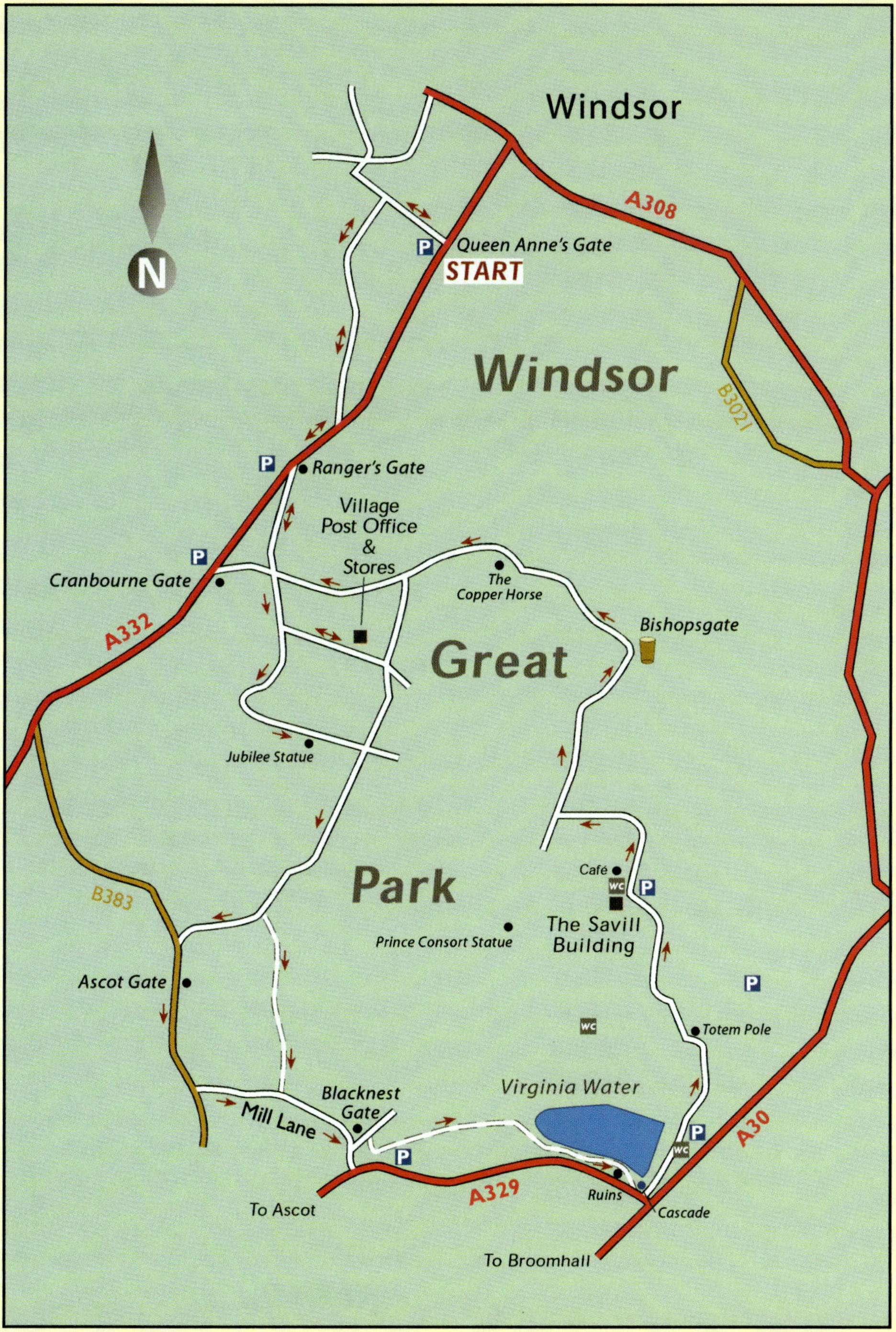

Windsor
A308
Queen Anne's Gate
START
N
Windsor
B3021
Ranger's Gate
Village
Post Office
&
Stores
Cranbourne Gate
The
Copper Horse
Bishopsgate
A332
Great
Jubilee Statue
Park
Café
WC
B383
The Savill
Building
Prince Consort Statue
Ascot Gate
Totem Pole
WC
Virginia Water
Blacknest
Gate
Mill Lane
A30
WC
A329
Ruins
Cascade
To Ascot
To Broomhall

*George III atop the Copper Horse*

building you can have lunch and perhaps explore the enticing shop and gallery.

Ride on from the gardens and stay on the main path as it bends sharply **L**. At a T-junction **turn R** through Cumberland Gate. Go straight on, past the junction signposted to the Village. Just before reaching the pink-washed Royal Lodge, the Duke of York's official residence, you can detour to the Fox and Hounds pub, leaving the park through Bishop's Gate on your right. The route continues through the metal automatic gates which are operated by a push button, high on a post to your left.

Glide down the hill, but prepare to stop when you can see the Copper Horse on your left, an equestrian statue of George III. To your right is a magnificent view of Windsor Castle down the Long Walk. Go straight ahead through the next automatic gates, where you will find the button to operate the gates high on a post on the right-hand side.

**Either: turn L** to the Village, if you are looking for tea and refreshments, and in about ¼ mile **turn R** to the Village store. Afterwards ride on from the store to the T-junction and **turn R**. Or: ride ahead to a T-junction and **turn R**.

Ride to Ranger's Gate. Cross the road and **turn R** on NCN 4 and retrace the outward route. This is straight ahead until you are about ¼ mile from the car park. Here you **turn R** back to Queen Anne's Gate.

## WINDSOR GREAT PARK

The Great Park, dating from the 13th century, consists of 5,000 acres of deer park set partly in Surrey and partly in Berkshire. It stretches from Windsor in the north to Ascot in the south and includes Virginia Water and the Savill Garden. Managed by the Crown Estate, the area is a wildlife and conservation area open to the public where a surprising range of leisure pursuits are permitted. Walkers, cyclists, fishermen, model aircraft enthusiasts, carriage driving and roller blading are all accommodated.

## VIRGINIA WATER

The vast lake of Virginia Water lies within the park and covers 120 acres. In 1746 the 1st Duke of Cumberland, victor in battle against Bonnie Prince Charlie, was appointed ranger of Windsor Great Park and had his soldiers dig a small lake. After it was destroyed by floods in 1768 a considerably larger construction, with an ornamental waterfall, began in 1780. Film crews have used the 4½-mile encircling path for filming certain lakeside scenes in the Harry Potter films, the Scottish version having proved unsuitable due to midges. The nearby Valley Gardens are home to an extensive and valuable collection of rhododendrons and azaleas and are ranked as being the finest woodland gardens in the country.

20

# Walton-on-Thames and Staines

## *14, 15 or 24 miles*

A gentle linear Thames-side ride in the north-west of the county which offers a relaxing option on a sunny day. The river from Walton bridge to Staines was described in 1910 by G. E. Mitton in his book, *The Thames*, as having 'a quiet prettiness', with 'placid green meadows, feathery willows, peaceful cows, and sunny little unpretentious houses'. Much of this remains true today. The short ferry ride from Weybridge to Shepperton and attractive Penton Hook Lock are highlights of the route but most of the ride is simply an enjoyable one beside the water. Extend your ride on the Thames Path eastwards and you can enjoy more delightful riverside riding and the charms of Hampton Court Palace.

**Map:** OS Explorer 160 Windsor, Weybridge and Bracknell (GR TQ093664).

**Starting point:** Walton bridge is on the A244. From Walton follow the signs to the bridge but turn left immediately before crossing it, into the large free car park.

**By train:** Staines station is about ½ mile from the route.

**Refreshments:** The Swan Hotel by the river in Staines, Thames Court pub on the towpath at Shepperton and the Kingfisher at Chertsey Bridge. If you take the short extension there is the Anglers right by the river on the way to Sunbury.

**The route:** An easy, flat, linear return route which, apart from a mile or two on a cycle track beside a road, follows the Thames. Cycling is on the main road when towpath cycling ends in Staines. However, you can push your bike along the towpath for ½ mile.

There is a pedestrian/bicycle ferry from Weybridge to Shepperton which runs every 15 minutes, summoned by ringing the bell. Last ferry 5.30 pm. Tel. 01932 254844 for further details.

From the car park **turn L** onto the towpath beside the Desborough Channel and ride for 1¼ miles passing D'Oyly Carte Island, previously home to Richard d'Oyly Carte, producer of the Gilbert and Sullivan operas. Just below Shepperton Lock there is a bell and steps to your right. Ring the bell, but it must be exactly on the quarters of each hour, when the ferry man will come and fetch you and your bike for a small charge. Once on the Shepperton bank, ride straight ahead for ⅓ mile and then **turn L** at the T-junction into Chertsey Road. **Turn L** at the B375 and cycle for a

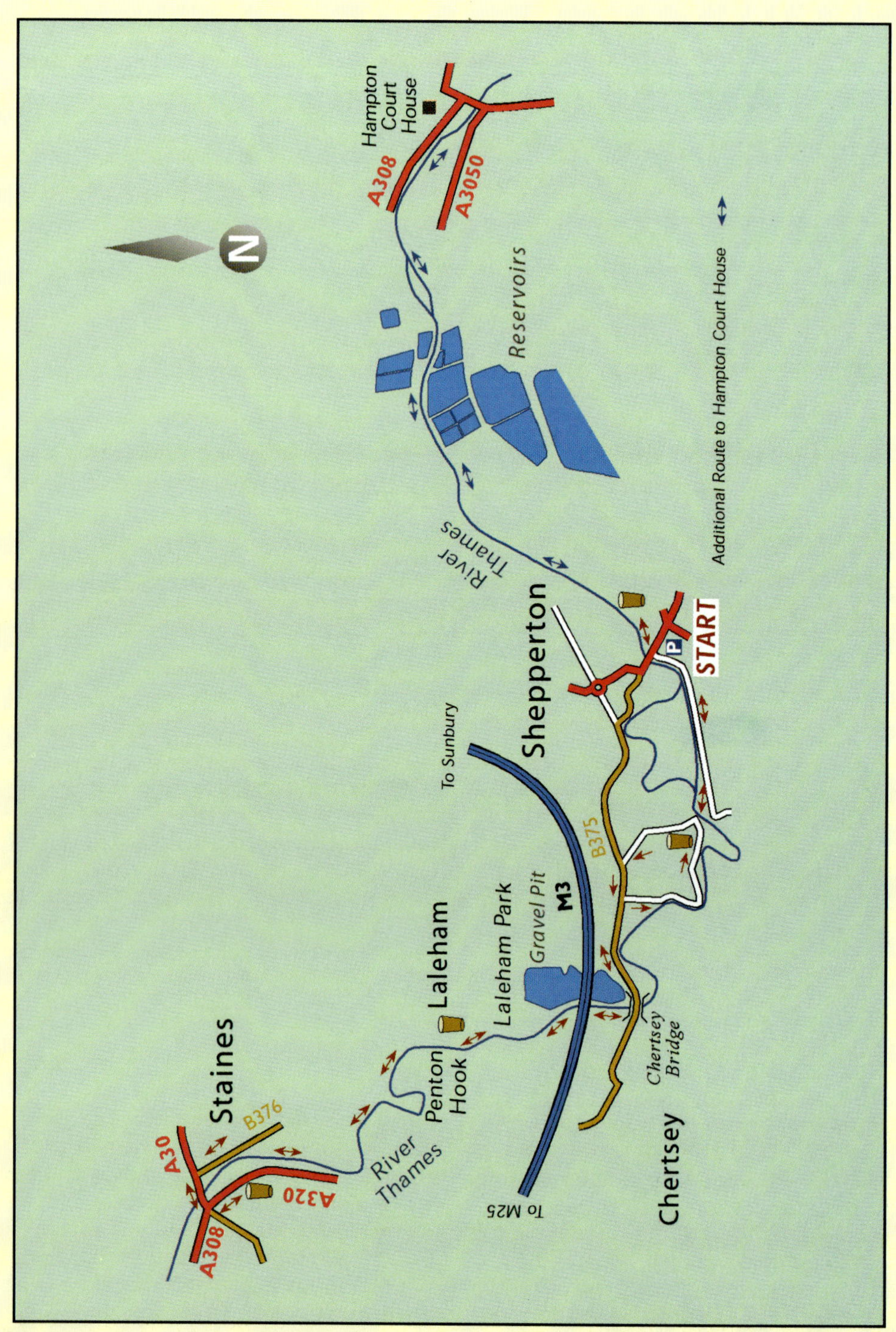

Hampton Court House
A308
A3050
N
Reservoirs
Additional Route to Hampton Court House
River Thames
Shepperton
P
START
To Sunbury
B375
M3
Gravel Pit
Laleham Park
Laleham
Chertsey Bridge
Chertsey
Penton Hook
Staines
B376
A30
River Thames
A320
A308
To M25

*A quiet stretch of the Thames*

mile, keeping ahead at the roundabout. You can use the pavement cycle track, the NCN4, on the far side of the road.

Pass the Kingfisher which is on your right near Chertsey Bridge and **turn R** beside it into Thames Side. You pass Laleham Park, once part of the grounds of Laleham Abbey, and in 1½ miles go straight ahead onto a pathway. In ⅔ mile you reach the beautiful area at Penton Hook Lock which makes a cut across a large loop in the river beside two weirs, one of which links to Penton Hook Island and the other to the disused part of the river. Consider a pause here to watch the boats in the lock, to admire the scene and perhaps to explore the small island where a nature reserve is being developed.

Ride onwards for 1½ miles across a grassy area and along the attractive riverbank towpath with small residential properties to your right. Where the cycle path ends in Staines, go to the road, unless you are opting for pushing your bike along the towpath. Maintaining your direction, go to Thames Street and ride along the High Street. The attractive Swan Hotel can be seen across the river. **Bear L** to cross Staines Bridge and **turn L** at the roundabout on the other side. The Swan is shortly on your left and makes a pleasant stop by the river.

Return across Staines bridge and **bear R**, shortly rejoining the High Street. To rejoin the river towpath, cross the road just after going under the railway bridge. Retrace the outward route beside the river. If you are feeling rather warm, then you may well seek an ice-cream van at Laleham Park, a mile or so beyond Penton Hook Lock. Continue to Chertsey Bridge, **turn L** by the Kingfisher and on to the roundabout. Cross straight over and ride on the pavement cycle track.

In just over ½ mile **turn R** into Dockett Eddy Lane, a one-way street and a departure from the outward journey. The road bends left with the river and soon there is the Thames Court pub with its attractive tables and umbrellas. Soon the return ferry from Shepperton is on your right. Ring the bell to return to Weybridge. **Turn L** along the Desborough Channel and the car park will be on your right just before Walton Bridge.

*Passengers alighting from the ferry*

To extend the route to 15 miles you can remain on the towpath at Walton, making a detour for ½ mile downstream to the Anglers pub. To make a 24-mile round trip and to visit Hampton Court, continue on the towpath from the Anglers for a further 4½ miles to East Molesey and cross the Thames at Hampton Court Bridge.

## STAINES

Staines is just within the Surrey boundary, although it used to be a part of the City of London whose boundary was marked by the London Stone. This was the marker for the boundary of the jurisdiction of the City of London, Staines Bridge being the next bridge upstream from London Bridge. The Stone is now in the Staines museum collection, attached to the library. A replica stands on the Lammas, the broad riverside recreation area north-west of Staines Bridge.

Although there is evidence that Neolithic people lived here between 4,000 and 3,000 BC, Staines really grew in importance in the year AD 43 when the Romans built a bridge to cross the Thames and named the large town that they built, Pontes. The river was wider and shallower then and was an important crossing point upstream from London on the way to Silchester, a large Roman town in Hampshire. Through the centuries a succession of bridges were built and then collapsed; for example, the bridge built in the 1790s lasted but one month! The foundation stone of the present three-arched bridge was laid in 1829. Although the bridge had to be widened to cope with traffic volumes it is the one that is still in use today.

## HAMPTON COURT

Cardinal Wolsey took over the site in 1514 and invested considerable sums in attempting to create a Renaissance cardinal's palace. His building forms the nucleus of the palace today. Fifteen years later Wolsey gifted the building to Henry VIII who in turn enlarged it enormously to transform it into a principal residence to house all the Court. William III had even more grandiose ideas and extended further in an attempt to rival Versailles. It is a palace of superlatives with a chapel, Tudor kitchens, state apartments, a maze and 60 acres of gardens, not to mention the ghost of Catherine Howard, Henry VIII's fifth wife, who is said to haunt the gallery.